FIDO Fundamentals In Dog Obedience
3rd Edition

Published By Robinson Dog Training
Written By Louis William Robinson Copyright 2016

ISBN-10:0-9981568-0-9
ISBN-13: 978-0-9981568-0-4

Contents

10

Louis William Robinson and "Cody"

Introduction

What happens when a Veteran K-9 Handler creates a dog training company that caters to pet owners? You get this book. I provide theory as well as technique that have been scientifically and effectively proven in not only the field but in everyday life. These are the same methods used by the United States Military to train K-9 warriors. Military Working Dogs are some of the most trusted and best trained dogs in the world. The methods in this book can be applied to any dog, any age and any breed. I strive to teach private citizens and K-9 handlers the immense benefits of understanding a dog's behavior and how it relates to training and behavior modification.

I hope that everyone who reads this book will gain valuable knowledge about the Principals of Conditioning (POC). These principals and training methods are used to teach basic obedience as well as advanced training. Upon learning these methods, you, the owner will be educated about POC and how it relates to behavior, training and obedience.

With a little patience and some guidance, you will be able to remove undesirable behaviors or substitute them with viable alternatives. Pet owners can finally learn to communicate clearly and effective with their dogs.

Louis William Robinson and "Leo"

Autobiography
Louis William Robinson

Louis William Robinson and "Orrie" 1998

I enlisted in the United States Air Force in October 1995 at the age of 18 and was sent to Lackland Air Force base for my Basic Military Training. During my time in Basic, I was given 11 additional Basic trainees to lead. Once I graduated from Basic, I was sent to the Ground Combat School where again I was given airmen to lead in addition to my daily duties. After being selected for Military Police school and again given a leadership role, I was hand selected based on rigorous testing for the very specialized career field of Military Police K-9 Handler.

I graduated from the 341st Training Squadron which is the joint military school for K-9 Handlers, where training is provided for the USAF, US Navy, Marines and a few select civilian police trainees. Some of whom may have been on a waiting list for a year or more. During my enlistment I was privileged to travel around the world handling military working dogs and assisted in training of both military and civilian police dogs. I have assisted with maintaining proficiency levels and retraining handlers to solve problematic canine behaviors. Dogs that I have handled have been chosen for additional "special duties "such as protection and detection for not only top secret or classified assets but also World Leaders. Those duties included both explosive detection and police/security duties.

After receiving an honorable discharge, I moved to Arizona to be closer to family. Life is too short to be wasting time doing things you don't love so I founded Robinson Dog Training and began training dogs privately. Since the inception of my company in 2007 I have worked with thousands of pets, their owners, working dogs, and their handlers. I am honored to be called "A leader in the K-9 Training Industry" by K-9 Cop magazine

Louis William Robinson and 'Sadie"

Bucket Brigade

Upon graduation from law enforcement school, I was immediately sent to K-9 school. The first few days were spent learning theory and application. To my surprise, when my class had gotten to the application of these techniques, we still had not earned the right to apply them to an actual dog. This is where  the term "bucket training" comes from. I remember the instructor making us wait in line for a bucket, then lining us all up in a field to practice drills. The idea of this is very similar to those of you who were made to carry an egg around in high school and pretend it was a baby. Because we only had book knowledge, we were not trusted with dogs yet. We had to learn and perfect the technique prior to being allowed to handle actual dogs. Each of us was issued a 5-gallon bucket and we were instructed to put rocks in the bottom. The instructor would bellow out an order and we were to command our buckets to comply (which they did not). "Sit" yelled the instructor. That was promptly followed by 12 soldiers commanding their buckets to sit in unison. He would then say "Your bucket did not sit!" in his raspy war hardened voice and we were to correct our buckets immediately. "Your bucket still did not sit!" he yelled and we were expected to reinforce the command to our bucket. We pulled up on our buckets with steady pressure while repeating the command "SIT." Finally, the instructor said "OK, now praise your bucket." As silly as this may sound we all did this until it became second nature, and we were allowed to handle actual dogs. We probably spent the better part of a week just learning how to properly train our buckets but it was worth it.

NOTE: It is important that your training technique be consistent to ensure maximum effectiveness. I highly suggest practicing the techniques on an inanimate object prior to applying it to your dog to ensure consistency of your method. If you are not consistent it will dramatically affect the number of "trials" needed to complete the training and confuse the dog.

"Bolt"

"Jax" and "Annie"

Gaining Behavioral Control

The ability to control a dog's behavior is a result of gaining stimulus control whether it's positive or avoidance (correction) based. The dog learns that a certain command or signal allows it to perform a certain task in order for it to receive a reward (praise, a favorite toy or food). You must be able to control the reward and it must satisfy the dog's needs. It also must be meaningful to the dog. Initial socialization training is designed to increase the value of vocal and petting praise. The dog must acknowledge vocal and petting praise as being of the highest value for rewards, which helps lead to greater behavioral control for the handler. It is also important to remember that the dog decides what the reward will be or it will not control the dog's behavior. Gaining behavioral control is also dependent upon using a reward schedule. You must perform the sequence properly by using the appropriate reward schedule or it will reduce the value of vocal and physical praise. The Variable Ratio and Variable Interval Reward Schedules will provide greater stimulus control.

Louis William Robinson and "Lucy"

"Zoey" 18 weeks

When to Start Training

Training is a constant and everything you do with your dog is training, one way or another. Be aware of your actions around your dog because your dog is aware of your actions. If your dog were to bark at the doorbell and you stroked the dogs fur in an attempt to get the dog to settle down and relax the opposite effect would occur because in reality the stroking is a reward for the behavior.

Dogs less than 14 weeks old should be trained using positive reinforcement and luring only. Dogs younger than 14 weeks are too young to use avoidance training on and should be trained gently. When your dog is 14 weeks old or older you may begin using the avoidance techniques outlined in other sections of this book.

When a dog reaches 2 years of age you can start working with off leash obedience drills assuming the team is already proficient on leash. As a general rule of thumb, older dogs tend to pick up new tasks at a faster pace because they are less distracted by external events like by butterflies and bumblebees.

Unless a dog is physically incapable of completing the desired task it is never too old to train. For instance, you would not train a 12 year old, husky to pull a sled. That would be like asking an elderly person to pull a truck. While there are exceptions, please know your dog's limitations.

"Tinker Bell"

RDT K-9 — ROBINSON DOG TRAINING PERFORMANCE EVALUATION FORM (DOG LOG)

Start Date:
End Date:
Your Name:
Dogs Name:
Dogs Age:
Dogs Sex:

Command List	Notes:
(C) = (Come)	
(S) = (Sit)	
(HS) = (Heel Stationary)	
(D) = (Down)	
(T) = (Stay)	

Weekly Results

Command	Start Time	Day	Trial 1	Trial 2	Trial 3	Trial 4	Trial 5	Trial 6	Trial 7	Trial 9	Trial 10	End Time	Notes:
		Day 1											
		Day 1a											
		Day 2											
		Day 2a											
		Day 3											
		Day 4a											
		Day 5											
		Day 5a											
		Day 6											
		Day 6a											
		Day 7											
		Day 7a											

Additional Notes:

Figure 1

Tracking Progress

Tracking progress is an important step in dog training and ensures that the dog is progressing as scheduled. The "Dog Log" forms (see figure 1) are at the end of this book and are designed for you to keep track of your progress.

In the Task collumn write down the command you are keeping track of for the week. The commands listed on the sheet are examples only. Feel free to track any commands you can think of. Then write down your start time and move to the first trial. Begin the trial by giving your dog the command.

If the dog responds correctly to the command the first time, then you will mark yes in the box by the appropriate trial number. If the dog does not respond correctly, apply a correction, either verbal or physical, and place a no in the appropriate box. This will complete trial 1 continue doing trials until you complete number 10. Finish your training session by writing the end time in the last section.

You will notice that during the training process the amount of "No's" will decrease as the training progresses. Keep the training sessions short in order to ensure the dog does not get bored.

I recommend a <u>minimum</u> of 2 short training sessions per day. The sessions should be between 5-15 minutes in length and never exceed more than 20 minutes at most.

The exception to this rule is training while out for a walk.

"Sabrina"

Feeding Schedules

Two common ways that dogs are fed are either a free feeding schedule or a set feeding schedule. With a free feeding schedule the dog's bowl is refilled when it gets low or emptied. Some people find this feeding schedule easier. There are a few draw backs to this method. The first drawback is that it is hard to control the amount the dog eats which may lead to excessive weight gain. The second drawback is that it makes it harder to tell if the dog is beginning to get ill. If a dog eats regularly, but suddenly loses its appetite it is a good indicator that the dog is not feeling well. The last reason to not free feed has to do with pack order; the job of a pack leader is not only to lead and protect the pack but also to determine how it's fed. Free feeding is not conducive to this because it does not assert your dominance.

A better alternative to free feeding is a set feeding schedule. This feeding schedule is the one that I recommend. When on a set feeding schedule try to keep feeding time around the same time every day. Ideally feed the dog after you eat to help assert your status as the pack leader.

Puppies that are between 8 weeks and 6 months old need to be fed 3 times day. After 6 months old, feel free to start feeding twice a day. You can switch from puppy food to dog food after the dog is done growing which normally occurs around 2 years of age.

Table scraps are ok assuming they are not dangerous for your dog but it should never be from off of your plate and always placed in the dog's bowl. If giving your dog leftovers it will ideally be done at a regularly scheduled feeding time, if giving the dog table scraps be sure to reduce the amount of dog food given during normal feeding time. Do not over feed your dog as this could make them not only fat but also sick.

"Coco"

Where to Sleep

People often get puppies and the first thing they do is let the puppy sleep with them. This is incorrect and may create pack order issues over time. An alpha, typically, takes the highest spot in the room in order to watch over the rest of the pack. The highest place in your bedroom that is suitable for sleeping is on your bed. A true alpha would never let a lower member of the pack sleep with it. By allowing your dog to sleep in your bed, you are not presenting yourself as the pack leader. If you need to cuddle up with something get a big fluffy pillow.

Did you know that most aggression cases have one thing in common; the dog has been sleeping in its owner's bed?

Instead of letting your dog sleep with you, it is more appropriate to let the dog sleep in its own bed, placed on the floor. If the dog is less than two years old, it should be secured in its kennel for the night. If the dog is already sleeping in your bed or has been recently adopted, expect the dog to cry for the first few nights when you put it in the crate. Ignore this behavior and it will normally go away within the week.

Did you know that dogs sleep more than humans? It is normal for puppies to sleep between 16 to 18 hours a day.

"Coal"

Training Equipment

Buckle collar

Every dog should have a buckle collar
in case you need to hang tags or
secure your dog. Buckle collars are
also the only collars that should be
used on puppies under 14 weeks of
age.

Leash

In the military, I used a 6ft.
long, braided obedience leash
that was ¾ of an inch wide and
made of leather. I prefer this
type of leash for obedience and

recommend these for many reasons but there are many
types of leashes that are suitable so pick one that you
like. I do not like retractable leashes because you may
run into issues applying a proper correction. Nylon
leashes are ok but with bigger and stronger dogs you
might get a "rug burn" if the dog sees a distraction and
pulls the leash through you grip. I have seen some
leashes that are made of chain but I feel they are too
noisy which can project your corrections and make
them harder to work with.

Proper Grip

If you have a 6ft leash and wrap it around your wrist several times then you should have bought a shorter leash. Not only is wrapping it around your wrist ineffective but it can also be dangerous. Imagine if you had a large dog and it wanted to chase something you may end up being dragged. Being able to let go of the leash is necessary for your safety. Not only is having the leash wrapped around your wrist dangerous but you limit the effectiveness of your correction with a traditional slip collar. If the chain is too tight, your dog cannot receive a proper correction because of poor range of motion.

For traditional obedience training with a slip collar, hold the leash in your right hand. This is assuming you are working the dog on the left hand side. The leash will hang across your body. The mechanics of the arm will enable the handler to get a better correction in this position.

When holding your leash put your thumb through the loop then grasp the leash between your pointer finger and thumb. It should be close to the dog with the clasp of the leash below the neckline. The excess leash should just hang. The extra slack is used if the dog pulls. The handler can then release some slack in the leash to ensure an open collar. This allows the handler to use the full range of motion for a proper snap. To properly utilize the above technique; you can practice on a tree, fence or another inanimate object. Attach the leash to a stationary object. Use the proper grip and practice going from a simulated pull to releasing and giving a good snap. If you learn this technique it will make training easier.

If switching to an electronic collar, hold the leash as described above but hold it in your left hand and the remote in your right hand.

House Line

A "house line" is a valuable tool for training which gives you the ability to catch or correct the dog when it does not have a regular leash on. To make a house line, find the thinnest nylon leash that you can find. It should be between 3- 5 feet in length and relatively low cost because you are going to cut the loop off of the end; ensuring that it does not get snagged on furniture or other objects. Attach the leash to a buckle collar for dogs that are less than 14 weeks old or use the slip collar if they are older.

There are many reasons to use a "house line". If a puppy steals your shoe and you chase it around the house, the puppy learns that all it has to do is take a shoe and you will take chase. This is not a behavior that you want to encourage so having a "house line" on the dog will make it easier to catch the dog and end the game. It is also important during time when you are just "hanging out" because you do not want to tell the dog to do something and not have the ability to make the dog follow through with the command. You cannot tell the dog to sit and let it wander off to the other room or the dog just learns it can ignore your commands. Remember everything you do with your dog is training!

Training collar/Slip collar/Choke chain

The equipment used in training is very important. Equipment that is ill-fitting or inappropriate will only make the training process more difficult. You want to use the equipment that applies as little force as is necessary to get the desired response from the dog. The training collar, also known as a choke chain or a slip collar is the most widely used type of collar for training purposes. Leave the chain on the dog for more than just training in case you need to correct the dog for behaviors you do not like. Never leave a dog unattended with one of these collars on as they may cause injury or strangulation if the collar gets caught on something. Imagine if your dog tried to jump a chain link fence in your back yard and got the chain stuck on it.

Never tie your dog up with a training collar, keep in mind that if you only use the slip collar for training, the dog may associate the collar with training. Leave the slip collar on while not actively training but the dog is attended to, so this negative association does occur.

Proper Fit

Neck Measurement

To measure for a proper fit, take a tape measure and place it where the collar will go. Measure as close to the skin as possible, keeping the tape measure snug. If the dog is very furry around its neck be certain to get the tape measure as close to the skin as possible. You want the collar to be the smallest size possible that fits comfortably over the dog's head. If you have a properly fitted collar, there should be enough room to get 1 finger under the collar of a small dog and 2 fingers under the collar of a large dog. Take the measurement 3 times to make sure your measurements are accurate.

Size

When choosing the correct training collar choose one that is well suited to the size of the dog. If your dog is larger than a Toy breed, choose a larger linked chain. Avoid collars made of small-link or jeweler's link chain; these are used only for small breeds. Some collars have a shoelace weaved in between each link which keeps fur from being pulled out. These are often called fur savers. Nylon slip collars are also available. They are easier on the coat and slide more smoothly than chain collars but do not make the same noise and may require more force to achieve the desired effect.

Chain Weight

Keep in mind that the weight of the chain is just as critical as the material it is made of. A heavy collar will quickly tire a small dog that is expected to carry the extra weight around for an hour or so. The size of the chain must be proportionate to the size of the dog.

Proper Length

When determining the correct length, the rule here is that when the chain is made into a noose it should slide comfortable over the dog's head without slipping over the dog's ears when his neck is bent toward the ground. If the dog leans forward and the collar can fall off over the head, it is too big.

Properly fitting chain on "Jake".

Correct placement

There is definitely a correct way and an incorrect way of putting a slip collar on a dog's neck.

Sit your dog facing forward on your left side. Make the collar look like the letter 'P' from the front view like in the picture. Slip it over the dog's head.

With the dog on your left side, the collar will instantly tighten and then automatically release when you quickly jerk the leash

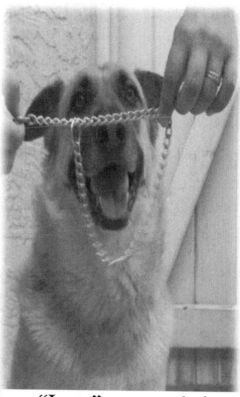

"Lucy" proper chain placement for left side

and relax. When the leash is incorrectly placed around the neck, the collar will tighten but not release properly when you issue a correction.

This is the type of training equipment that you should use when your dog is 14 weeks or older. With dogs is less than 14 weeks, use a buckle collar.

Alternative Collars

If you are not strong enough to apply a meaningful correction to your dog with a slip collar, you may want to consider one of these alternative collars. These collars will require you to use less strength, making it easier to apply a meaningful correction. I recommend a slip collar for most dogs. The majority of dogs do not require the use of these extra devices. Less strength is required with these tools so it is imperative that you have learned your technique and timing because you may create behavioral issues if your timing or technique is incorrect.

Prong Collar

Prong collars are also called pincher collars. They have a series of chain links with blunted open ends that turn towards the dog's neck so that when the collar is tightened, it
pinches the naturally loose skin around the dog's neck. The design of the prong collar is such that it has a limited circumference, unlike slip collars, which do not have a limit on how far they can constrict on a dog's neck. This collar is meant to simulate the mother dog biting the neck of her puppy for discipline. The collar is used to prevent the dog from pulling by causing pain and/or discomfort.

Prong collars can also be turned inside out with the prongs facing away from the dog's skin, rubber tips are occasionally placed on the ends of the prongs to protect against scratching or puncturing the skin. Some dogs may free themselves from prong collars by shaking their heads so that the links pop out. In this case you will want to use a buckle collar in addition to the prong collar.

Shock Collar

Shock Collars, remote training collars, e-collars, electronic collars and hunting collars are electronic training aids that were developed to deliver an electrical signal, vibration or tone through contact points attached to a dog collar. If using this type of collar with the CCRR technique (outlined later) **the device replaces the traditional snap of the chain** with an electronic correction. **You will still need to apply the reinforcement with a slip or buckle collar.** (Please see the CCRR section of this book for instruction on reinforcement.)

To properly fit a shock collar, make sure that the contact points are touching skin. If the collar is too loose, the correction will not be received when needed. If the device is on properly, it should feel tight enough that you can barely get a finger under the collar part of it. The placement should be on either the front or the side of the neck.

I rarely use the tone function and typically only use it to check if the collar is turned on. The instructions that come with collars say to beep prior to giving stimulation but for obedience I think the command should serve as the warning to increase command reliability. Tone could most effectively be used for a long distance recall so that you do not have to shout.

If you are going to be using a shock, it is of vital importance that your timing is correctly sequenced and paired with the word "NO", to prevent confusion. If your timing is not correct the dog will not make the proper association and you may actually make the problem worse. Ideally the dog will associate the correction coming from you and not some other source.

When using this type of collar as with all training collars you want to use the lowest level necessary to get the dog to respond. If the stimulation level is too high you will hinder training by causing fearfulness in the dog. Your correction should be hard enough that you can tell the dog received it but not so hard that the dog yelps. If the dog yelps on a low level the first time you issue a correction, don't worry. The dog may be startled, but if your dog continues to yelp after a few corrections you have your collar turned up too high.

There are many brands and types of e-collars on the market and I am not too particular but do prefer collars that are rechargeable and waterproof. I normally recommend using a slip collar on a dog but if you are not strong enough to apply a meaningful correction this may be a better alternative for you. Always learn your technique on a slip collar and only transition to this type of collar if needed. Never use this device on a dog that is less than six months old. If you find that your timing is terrible, I suggest contacting a trainer for assistance with this device, but it's your dog and you will have to learn the proper timing for successful training.

Another use for this device would be to train a dog to avoid specific behaviors like digging holes, eating poop, or jumping on a sliding door. When using an e-collar to break these habits the verbal correction is not required, simply give the dog stimulation during the undesired activity.

"Bill" and "Ted" Digging

"Sully"

Canine Basic Needs

A dog responds to its environment in order to satisfy its physiological (bodily) and psychological (mental) needs. A reward must be selected that can be controlled by the handler and also satisfy their dog's basic needs. Anything that satisfies a need but cannot be controlled by the owner will cause interference with gaining behavioral control and task performance, during all phases of training.

Oxygen
Breathing to obtain oxygen is the strongest drive of any animal. Unrestricted airflow after reinforcement can be considered a reward.

When the dog is worked or exercised, it will increase the dog's metabolism, which in turn increases the dog's need for oxygen.

Exercising the dog before training will cause a natural increase in the dog's breathing pattern (causing the dog to pant). This may interfere with training, in tasks requiring the dog to use its sense of smell.

Water

Water must be provided to the dog in adequate quantities to prevent thirst from interfering with the learning process or task performance. *Water cannot be used as a reward.*

Food

Food can be used as a reward, however; I typically do not use it for obedience training. The reason for this is because in most cases it is less reliable as a reward and harder to control over the other basic needs. If your dog is chasing a rabbit and you call him to come back and get some kibble, do you think the dog will come? If another basic need is a greater reward than the food, the dog can easily become distracted and unresponsive to the commands.

Prey Kill

Prey kill is an instinctive need for the dog to chase an object (like a squirrel) and to manipulate it (bite). *It is not always necessary for the dog to bite the object as the chase is part of the reward.* Manipulation involves the dog biting and tearing. A

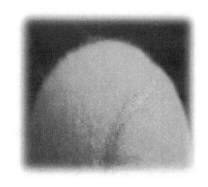

ball thrown or given to a dog during training can also fulfill this need and be can used as a reward.

Social Needs

Being pack animals, dogs, have a need for socialization. When a dog has been socialized to humans since it was a puppy, the dog will have the need to be with humans. Dogs' social needs are satisfied by both vocal and physical praise that is given by the trainer. A period of socialization between a dog and trainer is required in order for this vocal and physical praise to become meaningful for the dog as a reward. If the dog does not know the handler, the reward becomes less valuable. This socialization process must be continued for praise to be effective in maintaining some desired behaviors.

Minimization of Pain

The need to minimize emotional or physical pain is a basic need for dogs. Dogs attempt to avoid pain and painful situations. This basic need is manipulated in training to help keep a dog from making wrong responses.

Squirrel

Not too long ago, in a park nearby, two trainers were discussing who had the better trained dog. One trainer was a positive reinforcement only trainer from a major pet food retailer and used a technique, primarily based on treats and clickers. The second trainer used a combination of Avoidance and Reward training methods (outlined as CCRR in this book).

Both dogs flawlessly completed all of the basic obedience commands of "COME", "SIT", "HEEL", "DOWN", and "STAY" without distractions. They both did so well that the trainers tried to settle the competition with a series of more advanced training commands such as barking on command and retrieving objects but again both dogs performed well.

The trainers were about to give up when a squirrel darted across the park, in front of the dogs. The dogs were off leash and both gave chase. The first trainer pulled out some kibble and a clicker and yelled "COME". Unfortunately, the dog was too busy chasing the squirrel to pay attention and failed to return.

The second trainer called for his dog to "COME" but was also ignored. The trainer yelled "NO", immediately followed by the "COME" command and the dog broke off of the chase and returned.

(Eventually the squirrel got away and the first trainer's dog came back but not until the dog was ready.)

When reading this story, it is easy to see which trainer had the better results and which technique is more reliable. Let's take a look at why. With no distractions, both dogs performed well because the reward given for completing the desired task was sufficient for the level of distraction. Both food and social needs are basic drives so either can be used as a reward. The squirrel serves not only as a distraction but is also a reward because chasing it satisfies the "Prey Kill" instinct, which is a basic need.

Dogs choose the reward with the most value. The positive only trainers reward was not sufficient to get the dog to return. The second trainer's praise was not valuable enough to get his dog back either for the same reason, but this is where "CCRR" comes into the equation.

The reason the second dog came back after trainer yelled the word "NO" is because "Minimization of Pain" is also a basic need and it overrides other needs. This means that the need to avoid receiving a correction is more important than the reward of continuing the chase. The dog was off leash at the time but the dog still felt as if the trainer had applied a physical correction. This occurs through the use of a physical correction being applied in close association to the word "NO" and after enough trials when no physical correction is issued, it has the same psychological effect because the dog "feels" the correction even when one is not physically applied. When the dog "feels" the correction it is compelled to avoid receiving another and looks for a cue in order to avoid receiving another correction, thus eliciting the return.

Canine Learning Factors

Learning Acquisition

Learning is said to have taken place when behavior is changed relatively permanently due to practice or environmental experience. Changes in behavior that are temporary do not qualify as learning. The following are several terms a handler needs to keep in mind while learning to train dogs.

Extinction of wrong responses

This is simply withholding the reward when the dog makes no response or makes an incorrect response. Eventually the wrong response (or lack of response) will become extinguished and cease to exist. This process is shortened tremendously when the reward is of great value to the dog.

Stimulus generalization

This principle states that when a dog has been conditioned to make a response to a stimulus (command), similar stimuli (commands) may also evoke that response. If a dog is conditioned to respond to the verbal command of "down", similar words such as "clown or crown" may also cause the response.

Stimulus discrimination

The commands or cues that a dog learns must be very specific and consistent, in order to minimize stimulus generalization. Handlers need to realize that they are training dogs to respond on cue and not teaching the dog the English language. Dogs do not understand the specific words but know what the cue means, relative to a specific command that they are required to perform. Inconsistent cues will lead to confusion and inconsistent responses.

Positive Transfer

Positive transfer happens when what has previously been learned will compliment other learning. For example, a dog that has been trained to sit, in future lessons, is trained to sit in front of the door to go outside.

Negative Transfer

Negative transfer makes future learning more difficult. For example, during initial obedience training, upward pressure on the choke chain is a cue to the dog for the command to sit, which makes it confusing for the dog to later learn to jump when pulling up on the chain.

Cognitive Dissonance

Cognitive dissonance is the mental stress or discomfort experienced in the dog's brain when two or more contradictory commands are given at the same time or the dog is confronted with new information that conflicts with previous training. It will normally result in the dog's resistance to change. Picture a person who buys a puppy for protection training and the owner continually scolded the puppy for biting. This could later confuse the dog when trying to do protection (bite) work. This is not an unsolvable issue but something to be aware of.

Louis William Robinson and "Bruno"

"Sully"

Canine Sensory System

Auditory

This is the dog's ability to hear sound. A dog's sense of hearing is more sensitive than a human and they can easily detect noises at lower volumes and greater distances than we can. We use the dog's sense of hearing when we give it verbal commands and praise.

Vision

The dog's sense of sight enables it to see movement even during periods of darkness when it is difficult for humans to see. The dog's sense of sight also provides the dog with cues to learn a task. You use the dog's sense of sight when you give a hand command.

Olfaction

This is the dog's ability to smell. A dog's nose is its strongest sense and is said to be between 1,000 to 1,000,000 times more sensitive than a human nose. Imagine if all of the scent detection cells in your nose were laid out one after another they would fit inside of an area roughly the size of a dollar bill. If you were to do the same thing with a dog nose you would have an area roughly the size of a large handkerchief.

Pain (physical discomfort)

Physical touch relates to one of the dog's basic needs. The dog has the ability to detect different levels of pain as do humans. The other basic senses (like hearing a command) warn the dog of the impending onset of pain which in turn enables it to avoid the pain, or if the pain cannot be avoided, to minimize it.

We use the dog's sense of pain when we use the titration method in avoidance training. The dog will experience physical discomfort when we apply sharp, quick pressure on the training collar and just as quickly, release all pressure. By combining verbal corrections with physical corrections, the verbal correction will become emotionally uncomfortable to the dog even when a physical correction is not applied.

Pressure

The dog has several receptors which allow it to detect different levels of pressure. The dog senses light pressure through sensitive hairs that are called tactile hairs. These hairs enable the dog to feel changes in air pressure and pressure from wind direction. Light pressure also indicates to the dog a reward through petting praise. Receptors in the skin enable the dog to sense heavy pressure, such as the tightening of the training collar. The speed and amount of heavy pressure is a cue for the dog when used during escape or avoidance training. These behaviors will be addressed shortly. Quick heavy pressure usually indicates a correction such as a jerk on the leash.

Equilibrium

A dog's sense of balance enables the dog to maintain an upright position. The dog can learn to ignore the sensory input in order to accomplish certain tasks such as rolling over or crossing narrow objects.

Temperature

The dog has receptors that allow it to sense hot and cold. Walking on hot surfaces will inhibit learning during training. The dog can adapt to low temperatures with relative ease, but extreme cold temperatures will inhibit the dog's performance.

Body movement/position

The dog is aware of its body position and movement at all times. Receptors within the muscles, tendons, ligaments and joints send information to the dog's brain. This is important in training because the dog connects the reward with the last position of its body when the reward was given.

Taste

This sense allows the dog to indicate preference of one food over another. This is important if food is to be used as a method of reward for a specific task. I prefer not to use food rewards for obedience training. It is acceptable if avoidance cannot be used. Remember the dog will select the rewards value and there are often things that are more important to a dog than food which may impede using it as a reward.

Internal Receptors

These receptors enable the dog to tell when it is hungry, thirsty and when it needs to eliminate waste. These needs must be met or the ability to pay attention during training will be greatly diminished. The trainer must be aware and attuned to the way these receptors affect the dog's performance and must provide adequate breaks, water and food (unless you are using food as a reward).

"Cricket" and "Sakie"

Factors Affecting Senses

Several factors will affect the dog's basic senses. They do so by decreasing the recognition of sensory input.

Distractions

Distractions in an environment may confuse the dog or cause the dog to ignore cues given by the trainer. These could include people, other dogs, toys, vehicles, weather conditions or even a squirrel running by the dog during a training exercise.

Fatigue

Fatigue decreases the efficiency of the all the basic senses, especially when a sense is used for a prolonged period of time. A relatively short period of recovery time is required to bring the level of efficiency back up. Additionally, if the dog does not get adequate rest the basic senses will be adversely affected. Conversely, fatigue can be put to good use with active energetic dogs.

Disease and Age

These are the two greatest factors affecting the dog's basic senses. As a dog grows older, the visual and auditory systems become less efficient. Various diseases also decrease the dog's sensing ability, these two factors are considered together due to the fact that as a dog ages, it becomes more susceptible to disease. These factors are of a more serious nature than the others because the effects can be permanent.

Noxious Odors

Smells that humans find noxious, dead animals, skunks, or dirty shoes for instance may actually attract dogs and can be a huge distraction.

"Sasha"

Ivan Pavlov

Pavlov's Dog

Ivan Pavlov, a scientist that lived over 200 years ago, worked to unveil the secrets of the digestive system; he also studied what signals triggered related phenomena, such as the secretion of saliva. When a dog encounters food, saliva starts to pour from the salivary glands located in the back of its oral cavity. This saliva is needed in order to make the food easier to swallow. The fluid also contains enzymes that break down certain compounds in the food. In humans, for example, saliva contains the enzyme amylase, an effective processor of starch. Pavlov became interested in studying reflexes when he saw that dogs drooled even though it was not feeding time. Although no food was in sight, their saliva still dribbled. It turned out that the dogs were reacting to people in lab coats. Every time the dogs were served food, the person who served the food was wearing a lab coat. The dogs reacted as if food was on its way whenever they saw a person in a lab coat.

In a series of experiments, Pavlov tried to figure out how these responses were linked. For example, he struck a bell when the dogs were fed. If he timed the bell being struck in close association with their meal **(0 to .5 second)**, the dogs learned to associate the sound of the bell with food. After a while, at the mere sound of the bell, they responded by drooling.

Reflexes make us react in a certain way. When a light beam hits our eyes, our pupils shrink in response to the light, when the doctor taps you below the knee cap, your leg swings out. These reflexes are called unconditioned, or built-in. The body responds in the same fashion every time the stimuli (the light or the tap) are applied. In the same way, dogs drool when they encounter food.

Pavlov's' discovery showed how environmental factors that previously had no relationship to a given reflex such as a bell sound could, through experience, trigger the salivation reflex. This kind of learned response is called a conditioned reflex and is the process by which dogs and humans learn to connect a stimulus to specific reflexes.

Louis William Robinson and "Max"

Principals of Conditioning
*Please read this section several times until you grasp the concept.

Principals of conditioning are used throughout all phases of dog training. This means the dog receives a reward when he responds correctly and a correction when the dog responds incorrectly. Training must be continuous throughout the dog's life in order to remain proficient. The principles of conditioning as they appear in this material are not new. This information is a guideline based on scientific principles which enable a dog owner to evaluate a dog's behavior and plan a course of action to correct problem areas. These principles have been tried and proven. It is up to the owner to understand the knowledge and apply it to any situation.

Learn UCS, UCR, and CS

Classical Conditioning
Before we attempt to look at the aspects of classical conditioning, we first should look at some of the terms involved.

Unconditioned Stimulus (UCS)
This is a situation that naturally elicits a particular response. An example of this would be a dog hearing food being poured in its bowl, triggering a drooling response.

Unconditioned Response (UCR)
This is a biological reaction evoked by a UCS. An example of this would be a dog salivating when presented with food. To put these two terms into a formula we would see: UCS = UCR.

Conditioned Stimulus (CS)
This is a neutral stimulus that does not elicit any response until paired with a UCS. After pairing a CS with a UCS over several trials (20-40 times), a dog will

eventually acquire the ability to give the same CS response as with the UCS. An example: pairing the word "no" (CS) with a slip collar correction (UCS). *TIP: In order for this to occur the stimuli need to be paired at the same time or within 0.0 to 0.5 sec of each other.*

Conditioned Response (CR)

This is the response that is elicited by a CS, i.e.-slip collar correction. The response is similar to the UCR, but may not be identical. An example of this is a dog assuming there will be discomfort when there is no physical correction applied.

Extinction

Another important principle in conditioned learning is that an established conditioned response (salivating in the case of the dogs) decreases in intensity if the conditioning stimulus (bell) is repeatedly presented without the unconditioned stimulus (food). This process is called extinction

Classical conditioning is a simple form of learning that occurs when a neutral stimulus is used to bring forth a response that is usually caused by an unconditioned stimulus or in others words, pairing an unconditioned stimulus with a neutral stimulus until the neutral stimulus evokes the same response as the unconditioned stimulus.

An example of this can be seen in the training of the
bucket. Remember when I told you that each of us in
our K-9 handler training squadron was issued a 5-
gallon bucket? We were to command our buckets to
comply (which they did not). "Tell your bucket to sit"
yelled the instructor. That was promptly followed by
commanding our buckets to sit in unison (CR
expected).We were then told, "Your bucket did not
sit!" and we were to correct our buckets immediately, if
your timing was off by more than half a second you got
yelled at so, we told the bucket "No" with a quick snap
of the training collar (UCS/CS). "Your bucket still did
not sit!" We were expected to reinforce the command
to our bucket. We pulled up on our buckets with steady
pressure while repeating the command (CS) "sit".
Finally, (CR) sit. The instructor said "OK, now praise
your bucket." This becomes second nature when you
learn to train your dog as instructed.

"Kane"

Application of Classical Conditioning

When training a dog in obedience, classical conditioning occurs when a command is given ("SIT") and the dog doesn't respond. The trainer uses a UCS/CS (quick snap of the training collar when the dog does not sit, immediately paired with the word "NO") and the dog will learn to "SIT", CR when told to "SIT" to avoid the UCS/CS. These two stimuli are paired with each other over several trials. The dog then pairs UCS/CS with the command ("SIT") that will evoke a response automatically (the dog realizes it must sit immediately or experience a UCS/CS). **Conditioning occurs when the UCS and the CS are paired within 0 to .5 seconds of each other.** The CS is initially neutral and will not evoke a response until a sufficient number of trials are conducted. There are some considerations to be observed while using classical conditioning.

The UCR is a reflexive action that results in a response that the dog does naturally. It is automatic so there is no reward given in classical conditioning. However, if you continually present the CS (snap the training collar) without the UCS (saying the word "no") or the UCS (saying the word "no") without the CS (snapping the training collar), eventually the CR will not happen. An example would be to continually ring the bell without the food. Eventually, the dog will stop salivating at the sound of the bell; this is called the process of extinction.

"Gizmo"

Training Techniques

Avoidance Training

In this type of training the dog learns to make a response in order to avoid vocal or physical discomfort. When using avoidance training, a continuous reward schedule is followed. That is, every time the dog follows the command, it receives one reward. Once the dog responds reliably on this schedule, it will inform the trainer that the command is relatively resistant to extinction (not following the command anymore).

NOTE: If the reward is of sufficient value to the dog, it will select the right response in order to obtain the reward.

Escape Training

As the trainer applies pressure to the dog, the word "SIT" is requested of the dog. Once the dog assumes the correct position (dog sits) the pressure is released from the training collar and hips (positive reinforcement by removing the UCS/CS). As with other training, escape training has positive and negative effects on learning. Generally, dogs will yield to both forms of physical pressure and resist heavier forms of pressure (being too forceful with either the training collar and/or your body weight). Also, you must remember that pressure is a cue to the dog. The dog picks up a cue through its sensory system. These cues can work for you in all forms of conditioning. They can also work against you if they are incorrectly applied.

Luring

This type of training involves the use of positive reinforcement and is a relatively easy method to train the dog for basic tasks. The method is simply using a treat or other reward to guide the dog into the correct position. Luring can be used to make initial training easier but may not be as reliable as other methods. I suggest that if luring is used that the dog be eventually weaned off of the treats and the handler implements Avoidance and Escape methods to increase the reliability of training in the future.

Reward Training

The reward can be food, a special toy, or even praise depending on the dogs drive. With reward training, it is important that you have control over the reward and that you deprive the dog of this reward unless training. The dog will select the reward with the most value based on its drive.

Food Reward

This is the type of training you will often see at your local pet store (they sell dog food) or from most local trainers (it's easier to sell). It is often labeled as a kinder, gentler method of training and is sometimes called positive only training.

In the Air Force, it was used mainly for advanced training such as detection (finding a specific odor for reward). Food was most often used as a last resort for dogs that had low prey drive or low desire for socialization. When using food as a reward, it is advisable to reduce the amount of food given for regular meals and train enough to make up for the missing food. This means that the dog always needs to be hungry to increase the motivation for using food reward.

In the military, we needed our dogs to be as reliable as possible under all circumstances so we did not use it for obedience. If our dogs were not proficient, it could literally be the difference between life and death. The main problem with using food as a reward for basic obedience is that the dog can select a reward with greater value that may satisfy some other basic need.

I am not opposed to treat training but it has its limitations on reliability for obedience. Sometimes, food is used as a reward to teach advanced tasks for service dogs like picking things up or turning on the lights. Food reward can also be used to gain an aggressive dog's trust, but this is assuming that an adequate period of social deprivation has already occurred.

Toy Reward

When using a toy as a reward, it is important that you are able to control when it is given. This means that it should be a special toy and only used for training. The dog should not have access to the toy at any other time. We did not use toys for obedience training in the military, due to the reliability issues mentioned previously. Toys are preferred as a reward in detection training assuming the dog has a high "Prey Drive".

"The decoy or the person being attacked in protection training satisfies prey drive and can be considered a toy. "

Praise Reward

Dogs are pack animals and thereby social animals. This means we can use petting and vocal praise as a reward. This is my preferred reward method for basic obedience when used in conjunction with avoidance and escape methods.When using it in conjunction with avoidance and escape training; the dog learns it has two options. The first option is to be obedient and receive love and praise. The second option is to not comply, get corrected (avoidance training), get forced to do it (escape training), and then get praise (reward training). Most dogs will pick the path of least resistance and choose the first option.

"It is important to increase the desire for this type of reward through the use of social deprivation."

Marking Good Behavior (clickers)

I do not normally use clickers for training, let alone obedience training but since some trainers use it, I want you to know how it works. In order for you to become a good handler you must be familiar with all of the techniques available. Consider it another tool in your training repertoire.

This technique can be described as being based on the training principals, most commonly found in positive only reward training and is sometimes combined with the methods of training used in social deprivation. If you are going to be using a clicker or some other marker, the first step is to train the dog to associate the click with the reward which will most likely be food. In order for the association to occur the reward sound and the actual reward must occur simultaneously, or as near to it as possible. You have less than a second to make the dog associate the two stimuli as one. Repeat this process 20 to 40 times. Once this is done, you are able to use your marker for reward. Be careful not to use the marker too much without the food reward; otherwise, in 20 to 40 trials the association will disappear, according to the principal extinction.

To use this style of training, be on the lookout for good behavior and give the dog a sound reward when it does something you like which could be as simple as sitting or even just being relaxed. Be sure to pair the behavior with a verbal cue, such as "RELAX" and with enough trials you have taught your dog a new command. In the future, when you say "RELAX", the dogs' body should automatically respond.

When using social deprivation with this technique, you will simply go away and close a door for a few minutes when your dog acts up. An example of this would be if you caught your dog chewing on your boot, if you chase the dog around the house to discipline it, you are basically playing with the dog, thus rewarding and reinforcing the behavior. Instead of rewarding the behavior, you can use social deprivation. As you are walking away from the dog, call it to you and if the dog leaves the boot you can "Mark the Behavior". If the dog does not follow you, no matter how enthusiastically you try, then go to a different room and shut the door. The dog will learn that not only did it not get a reward but its human left too.

Remember, if you are using this method, the dog decides which reward is better. If the handler presents a piece of kibble to "COME" but the dog has a high prey drive, chasing the squirrel or chewing the boot may be a better reward.

Social Deprivation

Social deprivation is the technique used to increase the value of verbal and petting praise. When a dog is deprived of socialization, the animal is more willing to work for praise since this reward is a basic need. When using the social deprivation technique, contact with the dog should be limited to times when the dog performs a task for you, such as sit. Contact at all other times must be limited in order for this method to be most effective.

Counter Conditioning (fixing fear)

This is a method of training that is normally used to treat phobias (fears). If your dog had a negative experience resulting in undesirable behavior, counter condition can be a good tool to conquer this fear.

An example of this would be if your dog had its tail run over by a bicycle which resulted in the dog trying to run away every time a bike got close. To help the dog overcome this irrational fear, the handler will give the dog the reward every time it sees a bike, and after enough trials the dog will associate the bike with something positive instead, therefore, eliminating the fear of bikes.

With this type of training, the handler should first establish the minimum distance the dog reacts to the bike and start training from further away where there is no reaction. Complete at least eight trials at this distance and reward the dog immediately upon sight of the bike, if your timing is not fast enough, the dog will not make the appropriate association.

When the handler has completed enough trials for the dog to establish good things with the sight of the bike at the initial distance, reduce the distance by five or ten feet and continue training. Repeat this process until the dog no longer shows a fear of bikes.

If the handler increases the distance too much at once and the dog becomes fearful, go back to the last distance that the dog did not show signs of fearfulness and do at least eight more trials before attempting at a closer distance again.

"Bubba"

Veterans Day Parade Phoenix 2013

Method of Successive Approximation

This is a procedure by which you shape a dog's behavior through the process of moving from simple to complex tasks, in a series of steps (i.e.-sit, stay, long sit stay).

Final Response

Before any training can take place you must identify what the final response is going to be or exactly what you expect from the dog after it receives a specific command or stimulus. In some cases, you must show the dog the response for every command he is required to learn. Can you imagine a trainer showing a bird dog to point at a pheasant?

Titration

This method is simply using the lowest level of correction (vocal or physical) needed to control the dog's behavior. The important thing to remember is that this level is dog referenced. The dog determines for itself how severe the corrections are. Avoidance training should be used after the handler and dog have established good rapport, otherwise it will be ineffective. When using titration in avoidance training, if vocal corrections are not effective they are then paired with a physical correction. When vocal and physical corrections are applied, start with a normal vocal and low physical correction level. Increase the physical correction level gradually when the dog continues to make wrong responses. The dog's behavior determines the level of correction required for you to control its behavior. After a number of trials, the pairing of the vocal and physical corrections will allow the dog to avoid making an incorrect response, thereby, avoiding the vocal and or physical correction. Avoidance training gives the dog feedback that a response is incorrect but does not give the dog information on what the correct response is. Because avoidance training involves the use of emotional and physical pain, its use will reduce the value of praise. The trainer must insure that opportunities for praise are provided so that the corrections are balanced. If insufficient praise is given to counter the effects of the avoidance training, rapport will be degraded

One Trial Learning

Normally, training takes many trials depending upon the task. However, if one encounters a very strong stimulus, it can create a lasting impression and result in a permanent change in behavior. For example, if a handler stops a motorcyclist, presents the tail pipe of the vehicle for inspection to his dog and the dog burns its nose severely on the tail pipe causing a great deal of pain, the dog may (from that point on) attempt to avoid all motorcycles. Another example could be if you took your dog to the dog park and it was attacked by other dogs, your dog may become dog aggressive as a defense mechanism in order to scare other dogs away and prevent the occurrence of another traumatic event. This principal of training is used for Aversion training.

Snake Avoidance Training

Volume and Tone

When I work with clients they are always surprised that I maintain a low volume in my voice when correcting a dog. I do not want to have to yell at my dog for being disobedient so I train in a normal tone of voice. Dogs are all about associations, with this being said, it basically means that if I use a low tone of voice and correct with great timing then the volume of my verbal correction is relatively unimportant. The dog will make the association between the correction and whatever volume I decide to use. I prefer not to yell at dogs but I do like to say "speak softly and carry a big stick" (slip collar). I typically only raise my voice so the dog can hear me from a longer distance. Yelling at a dog in a combat zone when you are trying to not be seen is not a good idea.

Louis William Robinson and "Bosco" 1996

CCRR

CCRR is the most important acronym I can teach you. It stands for command, correction, reinforcement and reward. You will be best served to learn this and commit it to memory. All of our obedience training will be based on these four steps. To make sure you understand this, we will be using the sit command as an example.

Command

Issue the command of "SIT" in your normal tone of voice. If the dog responds and sits the first time, you will immediately praise enthusiastically. If the dog does not "SIT" then you will move to the next step in the sequence.

Correction

Say the word "NO" and simultaneously cause the chain to briefly tighten, be sure to let it release after the correction. Make sure that you pair the "NO" and the correction within 0 to .5 seconds of each other or the dog will not learn to associate the word "NO" with the correction. This is a very important step and may take practice but eventually the dog will learn that "No" is a negative consequence or an incorrect action. Once the dog has paired the physical correction with the word "No", you will be able to elicit the same response from the dog without the application of a physical correction. If the dog responds after the correction has been issued, praise immediately.

Reinforcement

If the dog is still not in the desired sit position, it is your job to teach the animal the correct position. To reinforce the command of sit, you will repeat the command while you apply steady, upward pressure on the slip collar while pushing down on the hind quarters. It is important to not release the pressure until the dog reaches the sit position. Once the dog is in the sit position, be sure to release the slip collar.

Reward

Congratulations - your dog is in the desired position. Enthusiastically reward the dog with lots of petting and praise or another reward. Get excited, raise the pitch of your voice and let him know he did what you wanted him to do. The more enthusiastic your praise the more valuable it becomes to the dog and the more likely it will increase the speed of the learning process. While rewarding, be sure to repeat the command so he associates the command, the body positioning and the positive attention with the last thing he did. Do not be afraid to look silly or goofy doing this, as it will expedite your path to success.

Training Restrictions

With any type of avoidance training there is a possibility for abuse, if the owner applies the training techniques improperly. Please remember that one correction per command is appropriate. Two corrections per command constitute punishment. Three corrections per command is dog abuse. Four corrections per command are aweful and someone should call animal control on you because it is cruel and you obviously did not read the entire book. That's a little military humor for you.

Timing

Timing is one of the most important factors when it comes to dog training. When you first issue the command, give the dog 3 – 5 seconds to respond before applying a correction.

If the correction is issued, make sure you pair the word "No" at the same time the correction is applied or within half of a second. The dog will pair the verbal and physical correction if the timing is correct.

Give the dog another 3-5 seconds to respond after applying the correction prior to reinforcing the command.

The reward should be given immediately upon correct completion of the command so the dog will learn what is expected.

NOTE: Timing is extremely important in avoidance training. It must be given with a sudden quick onset or you will "telegraph" the correction to the dog and he will take actions to avoid or minimize the pain. Also, vocal and physical corrections are given only during the time the dog is in the process of making an incorrect response. Corrections at any other time do not provide the dog efficient learning cues.

Louis William Robinson and "Sadie"

Practice

I am not going to ask you to get a bucket and train it but I am trying to get the point across about how vital the proper timing is. If you have to think about what the next step is, you took too long. You want this to be entirely second nature or in other words, reactionary. The only way this is going to be accomplished is through practice and repetition. I strongly suggest that you take the chain and slip it over your foot or some other inatimate object. This can be done either standing or sitting in a chair. Practice the timing of the

command, correction, reinforcement and reward, until you no longer have to think about what comes next. Practice at least 2 times a day for a week or until you can do it seamlessly. Once you perfect this technique you will be ready to apply it to the dog

Obedience Training Techniques

Congratulations - You are now ready to apply these techniques to your dog. All of the commands will follow the four steps you have just learned, except for the "drop it" command which we will go over in more depth further down the page. Remember CCRR and that there should be a pause of 3-5 seconds between the Command the Correction and the Reinforcement. Take your time with this and remember to keep track of your progress. You will want to start with one command a week or until the dog responds correctly 100% of the time before moving to the next command. Initially, all commands must be done on leash.

OUT/DROP IT

If you teach this command to your dog properly, you will be able to make your dog spit out a variety of things, both high and low value 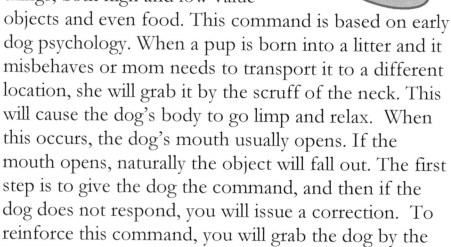 objects and even food. This command is based on early dog psychology. When a pup is born into a litter and it misbehaves or mom needs to transport it to a different location, she will grab it by the scruff of the neck. This will cause the dog's body to go limp and relax. When this occurs, the dog's mouth usually opens. If the mouth opens, naturally the object will fall out. The first step is to give the dog the command, and then if the dog does not respond, you will issue a correction. To reinforce this command, you will grab the dog by the scruff of the neck and gently lift until the dog releases. Once the dog releases, lower the dog and praise. If the dog yelps, it is not hurt, it is just objecting to the discipline but the item in the dog's mouth will fall out when the dog does this. If you find that you have a stubborn dog that does not release when you have all four feet off the ground, give the dog a gentle jiggle. DO NOT GIVE YOUR DOG SHAKEN BABY SYNDROME. The proper place to grab is in the middle of the neck but for stubborn dogs try moving your grip further down the spine. If doing this with an older dog or unfamiliar dog, replace the scruff grab with steady pressure from a slip collar.

COME

Give the dog the command "COME". If the dog ignores you or is distracted, apply a correction. If you need to reinforce the command after the correction, then reel the dog in like a fish. Pull your dog straight to you maintaining steady pressure and repeat the command "COME". When the dog reaches you, be sure to release the pressure and reward. It can be helpful to crouch into a lower position and remember never correct the dog when it arrives to you or it will make the wrong association.

SIT

The dog receives an upward correction for not responding to this command and the reinforcement is steady upward pressure while pushing down on the hind quarters. Release the chain and praise the dog for reaching the desired position.

Boundary Control

The pack leader controls entry and exit. My dog will not leave the front door without permission, even if I am not there. In order to achieve this have the dog on a leash and chain and open the door, allow the dog to attempt to walk through the boundary. When the dog reaches the threshold of the boundary and attempts to go through, issue the dog a correction and pull the dog back in, close the door and repeat. After a few attempts, the dog will stop trying to get through and look at you when you open the door. When this occurs, you tell the dog to sit. Once the dog is sitting, face the dog and back through the doorway slowly. If the dog breaks position and tries to go through the door again, issue a correction and the command to sit, repeat these steps until the dog stops trying to get out. Once out of the door, call the dog to you. When the middle of the dog's body crosses the threshold of the boundary, you will tell the dog to "SIT" again so that when the command registers in the dog's brain, it is sitting just outside of the door. Now you may close the door and lock it without the dog dragging you down the street for a walk. This process needs to be repeated upon entering the doorway also. Once your dog is good at one door, begin adding other doors. This technique will only work on doorways that you practice it on. So train for boundary control on yard gates, back doors, cars doors and any other place you might want or find useful.

HEEL (walking)

Start walking with your left foot first and give the command "heel". This will serve as a cue for your dog to begin walking. In the proper position, the dog chain should be even with your shins or slightly behind you. "Nose and Toes" is to remind you to keep the dog's nose behind your toes. As soon as your dog gets ahead of this position issue a correction to the right assuming the dog is on the left or in the opposite direction of the dogs pull but don't slow down or stop walking because this could be a cue for the dog to brace itself and mitigate the correction. If the dog does not respond then reinforce while repeating the command with steady pressure to a position slightly behind the correct position, release the chain. The act of walking is a reward for a dog so keep on walking and keep in mind that excessive praise may be a distraction

Heel Postion

Correct "HEEL" Position

Incorrect "HEEL" Position

HEEL (Stationary)

Stand still and give the command"HEEL". The dog should come and sit next to you on your left side facing forward. In order to teach this command, get the dog into any position that is not correct and move yourself away. It is imperative to get the dog out of the correct position before starting. Once you reach the end of the leash you will give the dog the command of "HEEL". Correct towards the desired position and reinforce with steady pressure by pulling the dog and placing it into the correct place while maintaining the steady pressure. Once the dog is in the desired position, be sure to give it praise. This is one of the most difficult tasks for dogs to learn in the basic obedience regimen and may take longer than the other commands to get accomplished. Do not get frustrated, your dog will get it over time. People ask me all the time "Does the dog know the difference between Heel Walking and Heel Stationary?" The answer is yes. The dog knows if you are walking or standing still and can tell the difference between the two.

HEEL (High Collar Technique)

This technique is used to make a dog that is not that well trained keep pace with the handler and keep its head up. You will often see this in dog shows where the dogs are judged based on physical appearance. These dogs are not always handled by their owners and are often not trained very well. Even though they are not trained well, they still have to put on a good show for the judges. This technique uses the principal of reinforcement only; there are no corrections with this training. DO NOT CORRECT THE DOG IN THIS POSISTION. In order to accomplish a proper high collar technique, slide the chain up the neck until it is under the jaw. The handler will hold the leash straight up from this position, forcing the dog to keep its head up. The collar should be loose but still held high when the dog is in the right position and the dog should feel slight pressure when it is too far ahead or slightly behind. The handler is not trying to choke the dog with this position, only train the dog to walk in the right spot. Be sure to repeat the command "HEEL" or whatever command you are using while the position is being reinforced.

High Collar Technique

Marching Drills

These exercises are used to teach the dog to follow the movements of the handler when changing directions. The commands can be directional if you choose such as "LEFT", "RIGHT" and "TURN". This training is all about commands and reinforcement. There are no corrections issued during these maneuvers. When holding the leash, be sure to only give the dog enough slack so that it is comfortable for the dog when it is in the <u>correct</u> "HEEL" (walking) position. These commands are initiated while you are already walking with the dog; don't start from a stopped position.

When turning left, your movement should be a sharp 90 degree angle and say "LEFT" when you are turning. If the dog is in your way, bump the dog out of the way with the swing of your left leg or knee, depending on the height of the dog. Eventually, the dog will start watching out for your left turn.

When turning "RIGHT" it should also be a sharp 90 degree turn. If you are handling your leash correctly, it will get tight as you turn if the dog falls behind and when the dog gets into the correct position, the chain should again be loose.

When doing the "TURN" it moves the same as "RIGHT" except it is a 180 degree turn. This drill should only be implemented after the dog is proficient with "HEEL" (walking). The hardest part of this drill for most people is learning to march.

Please practice marching without the dog first before adding this routine to your walks. Do not forget to praise your dog when it is in the proper position.

DOWN

The dog receives a downwards correction for non compliance and the reinforcement can be applied in one of two ways. To apply the reinforcement, while repeating the command you may either pull down on the chain with your hands or you may place your foot where the chain and leash connect while forcing your foot to the ground. Once the dog is in the down position, release the pressure and praise.

Reinforcing "DOWN"

STAY (Basic)

It is important to only increase one variable at a time. You will need a stopwatch or a clock with a 3rd hand for this. Start by putting the dog into the stay command and gently tapping on front of the nose. Move to the end of the leash and wait until the dog breaks the position. Pay careful attention to the time it takes for the dog to break and decrease the time by 5 seconds. Now that you have a starting time, it will be easier for you to track progress. If the dog leaves the position you left him in, correct while moving into the dog and reinforce verbally with "STAY" and moving the dog back to the same spot it was in when you gave the initial command, while applying steady pressure to the slip collar. Once the dog stays in the desired spot for the target time, call the dog to you and praise enthusiastically. Repeat this exercise until the animal has a proficiency of 100% at that time and distance. After this has been accomplished then increase the length of time required or the distance between you and the dog but do not increase both variables the same time. The variables should be increased in small increments. If you find yourself correcting the dog more than rewarding it, you should decrease the variable to last known reliable trial.

STAY (Advanced)

When the dog is proficient at "STAY", start implementing larger distractions such as throwing toys or food nearby while in a "STAY" and be ready to correct if you have a dog with a high food or prey drive. It is a good idea to have a helper assist with these drills by throwing the toys or walking around the dog. Never use a toy associated with reward for advanced training with a working dog. The dog can watch the object but cannot break position.

Another popular advanced stay drill is to leave the dog in a stay position while the handler moves out of sight. In order to do this drill, you will want to use the corner of the wall so you can simulate being further away than you actually are. Tell the dog to stay and move out of sight. Stay close enough that if your dog moves, you can hear it and move around the corner to give the dog a correction. Other drills include walking around the dog, straddling the dog, and stepping over the dog. Before doing these maneuvers a handler should give the dog the "STAY" command again prior to moving as the dog may think the drill is over if the handler moves before repeating the command. The drill is over when the handler calls the dog or begins to praise.

LONG LEASH (Distance Training)

Long leash training is to make the dog more proficient at longer distances. Start with a ten feet lead and keep working your basic commands until the dog is proficient at ten feet then move to a 15 or 20 feet lead and continue working until the dog is good at the new distance. These longer leashes are much harder to work with and will take practice but don't give up, it will be worth it.

Long Leash training

OFF LEASH (Off Leash Training)

A good handler can maintain control over his dog without a leash if properly trained. Off leash training should not be attempted with a dog less than 2 years old because they are still easily distracted which can hinder training.

Step one is to make sure the dog is 100 percent reliable at long distances.

Step two is to use a 6 feet lead and work obedience commands while not holding the leash but still attached to the dog. This is called "DROP LEASH".

Step three comes when the dog is proficient at drop leash with 100 percent proficiency on all obedience commands. Once this is accomplished, you can try off leash in an enclosed area. Welcome to off leash training.

In the military, some dogs needed a "cheater lead" which was basically a regular weight leather leash only 3 or 4 inches long to make the dog feel as if it still has a leash on.

Off leash training is a goal for many pet owners but please check local leash laws before attempting this in public. Always be aware of your surroundings before starting and do not attempt off leash training until your dog is reliable with all commands.

"Bruno"

Reward Schedules

Continuous Reinforcement (CRF)

This is a schedule in which every correct response elicits a positive reinforcement (+RF). Every time the dog makes a correct or near correct response, it receives a reward. Assisting the dog to assume a particular position (escape training) is permissible but only reward the dog while it is in the correct position. Shaping the dog to make the correct response will require a slight delay in providing the +RF. An excessive delay of reward will not assist the dog to learn a task. Use the method of successive approximation for this process. This type of training would be utilized when the dog has learned a new task but is not yet 100% proficient in its completion.

Extinction

In classical conditioning, extinction results when the conditioned stimulus is no longer paired with the unconditioned stimulus. In operant conditioning, it is the gradual disappearance of a response as a function of the withdrawal of reinforcement. In other words, if the dog makes no response or an incorrect response to a stimulus, no reinforcement at all is given. When this happens the dog should be given the command again to elicit the response. If the dog still does not give a positive response to the second attempt, then redefine the final response using escape training. The use of the extinction schedule in conjunction with the continuous reward schedule, in initial training, provides information to the dog. He learns the right response from the wrong response. If the reward is of sufficient value to the dog, it will select the right response in order to obtain the reward.

Fixed Ratio (FR)

This is a schedule of reinforcement in which a predetermined or fixed number of responses must occur between each of reinforced responses. The responses do not have to be from the same stimulus. Example, first give the dog the verbal "SIT" command and when the dog sits the next stimulus is provided. Let's say you give the "DOWN" command. If the dog lies down it has now completed a fixed number of responses. To start a dog on this schedule, for every two correct responses the dog makes, it will receive one reward. When the dog reaches 100% proficiency at this rate, the next highest ratio is utilized.

When working on this schedule, it is important to vary the order of commands or the dog will associate the second command with the first and will complete the second command automatically when hearing the first command. An example of this can be seen when an owner begins working on the down command. I frequently meet with owners who have dogs that lie down every time they are given the command to sit. This occurs because the dog was on an (FR) schedule of 2:1 and always did the "SIT" command prior to doing the "DOWN" command.

Variable Reward Schedule (VR)

The variable reward schedule or (VR) is the next step after a dog is proficient on a (FR) schedule of at least 3:1. On a (VR) schedule the dog performs a random series of tasks but no more than the highest number of commands on the last (FR) schedule. This will ensure the dog does not know when the reward will come and will be more willing to perform multiple commands. This schedule should be used in conjunction with a (FR) schedule.

Fixed Interval Reward Schedule (FI)

This is a schedule of reinforcement in which a predetermined $(x=d1)$ or distance interval must occur between each reinforced response, regardless of the number of responses made. In the (FI) reward schedule when the dog has made a response for a fixed period of time or distance, it is given a reward. In initial training, a short period of time or a short distance must be selected. When the dog performs at the 100% proficiency level at that time period or distance, increase the time or distance at which the dog must make a response before it receives its reward. Again, we use the method of successive approximation when moving from simple to complex, to achieve this goal. The periods of time involved in the increase should be relatively short (for example 5 seconds) and the distance increases should also be relatively short (3 to 6 feet). When the dog reaches 100% accuracy, at that level, increase it to the next level and so on until the maximum level is reached. As in the FR, if the dog does not respond correctly at one level, decrease the time or distance until he reaches 100% accuracy.

NOTE: Distances and time intervals that are provided in this study guide work book are only guidelines. Some animals may be able to tolerate the use of greater time and distance intervals than suggested and some may not. Remember if the dog fails to perform at any point, decrease the interval to the last known point where the dog performed at 100%, and do 8 more trials before attempting to increase the interval again.

Variable Interval Reward Schedule (VI)

This schedule of reward provides reinforcement following the first correct response after different intervals of time or distance. Once the dog has learned to perform any task at a specific distance or for a specified amount of time on the (FI) reward schedule, you may begin the (VI) schedule. The maximum length of time or greatest distance that the dog is required to respond on this schedule, must have been attained at the 100% accuracy level on the (FI) reward schedule. When using a (VI) reward schedule, select a time range (example 1-2 minutes) or the system becomes less efficient.

NOTE: When conditioning a dog for task performance in operant conditioning, the dog will always be on more than one reward schedule at one time. For example, the dog may be on a (FI) of 3:1 and on a (VI) of 10 to 20 seconds. One thing to remember, however, is that you increase the levels for each schedule one at a time. To increase more than one at the same time will confuse the dog. The use of continuous reinforcement and extinction schedules is done primarily during initial training phases because they provide the dog with the maximum amount of information on the correct response. The Schedules that provide the most behavior, control and flexibility are the (VR) and (VI). This is because the dog receives information, the correct response on a random basis at a varied period of time. The dog is never certain when the trainer will give the reward. These two schedules also make it difficult to extinguish an undesirable response. Because the dog is not receiving a reward for all the correct responses, merely withholding the reward for an incorrect response does not provide the dog with the information that it was not a correct response. This is the reason why detector dogs are trained on the continuous reinforcement and the extinction schedules.

Additional Training

Name Recognition

Training a dog to know its own name is one of the first things you should work on. This training does not need any corrections and is positive based. Take the dog on leash to an area with minimal distractions and tether the dog to yourself or a stationary object using your buckle collar to avoid restricting airflow. Say the dog's name when it is looking at you and praise the dog. You may use treats if you like but verbal and petting praise should be sufficient. There are no corrections involved with name recognition training as it should be all reward based. If you adopt a shelter dog, this technique can also be used to rename the dog.

House Breaking & Crate Training

These two things go hand in hand and can be trained simultaneously. First, let's talk about **CRATE TRAINING**. Dogs are considered "den animals", this means if they were out on their own in the wild they would create a den to live in that would be big enough for the dog to stand up and turn around in. With that being said, your crate should be approximately the same size.

Crate training should always be a positive experience. When putting the dog in the crate, you can lure the dog into the crate with a toy or food and be sure to give the dog a command for the action such as "CRATE",

"KENNEL", or "HOUSE". A lot of people will place bedding into the crate but unfortunately this can become a health hazard for dogs that are still in the destructive stage of life which is for most dogs under the age of two. They could potentially swallow a piece of bedding and get it stuck in their Gastro Intestinal Track causing blockage that may require surgery. Never put a food bowl or water in the crate because it is detrimental to potty training since it will be harder for the dog to control its bodily functions over a prolonged period of time. Remember, what goes in has to come out. Placing one toy in the crate is acceptable but more than that may not give the dog enough room to lie down. Never let the dog out of its kennel while it is making noise, this will only reinforce the behavior, making it worse over time and before you know it, you will have a dog that tries to chew its way out its crate. Instead only let the dog out while it is quiet and content. Do not use your crate for a "time out"; otherwise, the dog will begin to associate it with negative things when in reality the crate should be a happy and safe place. Leaving your dog in his crate overnight is acceptable and during the day I would recommend trying to get the dog out of his crate for a potty break every 4-5 hours. Remember with smaller and younger dogs they need to potty more often as they have smaller bladders and will need to eliminate more frequently. A lot of people think that crate training is mean but in reality it is one of the best things you can do for your dog.

Potty Training

In order to potty train your dog, you should crate train the dog at the same time, this will make training easier. With potty training, you are going to use both avoidance training and reward training. Dogs are relatively clean animals and most of them will try not to lay in their urine or feces, we can use this instinct to our advantage by only giving the dog enough room to stand up and turn around. If a crate is too big, the dog can eliminate in one part of the crate and lay in another which will greatly hinder training. Large breed puppies will outgrow their kennel if it is properly sized. Most puppies will need to eliminate about 20 minutes after eating or drinking. They will also need to eliminate after playing and taking naps. This will give you a good idea of when your dog has to eliminate waste. Keep young dogs on a leash, always in your direct line of site if they are out of their kennel. Always look for any signs of needing go to the restroom such as sniffing around, squatting, or lifting a leg and immediately take the dog to an appropriate spot on leash and praise heavily once the is dog finished. If you catch the dog after it has gone to the bathroom someplace it shouldn't then it is too late to correct the dog for the action. If you give the dog a command while eliminating such as "BREAK" or "POTTY" later you will gain control to some extent of when the dog relieves itself.

Relax it's just mud

The old idea of rubbing the nose in the mess does not work and will only confuse the dog further. In order to correct a dog for an accident, the correction must occur at the time of the incident. You only have half a second or less for the dog to make the correct association. If you want the dog to go in a specific area, be sure to take the dog only to that area and correct all other areas. Most dogs can be potty trained in less than 30 days if done properly.

Hand Signals

In the military, we use hand signals because it is not always wise to yell commands at your dog when you want to be silent. Hand signals are easy to teach and they can be taught at the same time as your regular obedience commands or after the dog is already proficient at the commands. Make sure the dog is looking at you when you give the command verbally and gradually reduce the number of times the command is issued verbally while using had commands consistantly. Make sure your hand commands are different for each command and stay consistent with them.

Other Languages

Clients frequently ask if police dogs are trained in other languages to prevent people, other than their handler, from giving the dog commands. This is a myth. A working dog will not let go of a bite because the bad guy yells to let go, regardless of the language. The reason that some working dogs are trained in other languages is normally because they are purchased from a country where that language is used. Dogs don't understand language, they respond to commands and cues from their handler. Any language you use for training will be fine as long as the dog is able to tell the difference between the commands. If you have multiple dogs, consider training each dog in a different language to give you more control over each dog independently.

My dog knows three languages; she knows English, German, and hand signals. When she was first trained she learned in English and hand commands simultaneously. When she was proficient with those, I eliminated the verbal cue and went to hand commands only. When she was at 100 percent with the hand commands, I started using German while doing hand signals; eventually, I dropped the use of the hand signals and only used German. Before I knew it, my dog was trilingual.

Place

Training a dog to go to its place can be done relatively easily with a slip collar. First, you will need a mat, rug, dog cot or otherwise suitable item for the place. Lead the dog over to the matt and praise heavily while repeating the command place. The dog should be familiar with "PLACE" after a few dozen trials. Then try it from a few feet away with a leash and slip collar; if the dog does not go to its place, give the dog a correction and wait a few seconds, if the dog does not go to its place then lead the dog over with steady pressure and release the pressure when the dog is in the place. When training for place, initially, keep the time required on the mat short and gradually increase the time on the place using a Continuous Reinforcement schedule and eventually work towards a Variable Interval reward schedule.

Luring can also be used with this command. In order to use luring guide the dog onto the mat with a treat while giving the command. When the dog reaches the correct place give the dog the reward. Gradually increase the amout of time in the place and reduce the treats over time.

Remember that anything can be used as a cue for place. I met an elderly couple that had limited mobility. They had three young dogs that were super excited to meet new people and jumped all over them. They did not want their dogs to jump on guests. Due to their moblity issues they had a hard time controlling the young dogs when the doorbell rang. The solution to this problem was to use the doorbeall as a cue for place. They trained each dog individually to go to its own matt by the door. One person would be outside of the door to ring the bell for the cue and one person would be inside to guide the dog. After the training was complete you could ring the doorbell and all three dogs would go to their place, until released. Be creative with your training.

Fiona in "PLACE"

Nipping (No Biting)

Puppies love to nip. This is how they explore and interact with the world, unfortunately, they have sharp teeth. This training can be accomplished with a combination of the following methods; reward, avoidance, or extinction through social deprivation.

Louis William Robinson and "Lucy"

For the reward method, use a praise, toys or treats. First, tell the dog "no biting" and slowly withdraw your hand from his mouth. If you move too quickly you incite the Prey Kill drive and the puppy will chase your hand. Prey Kill drive satisfies a basic need and is reward, so don't pull away. Instead remove your hand slowly and distract the pup with a toy. Your puppy will learn to play with toys to satisfy this need.

If your puppy is food motivated, hold a treat in your hand and keep your fingers tightly clasped. If he bites to get the food, do not open your hand. When the dog is not biting and takes his mouth off your hand, give him the treat and praise.

To use avoidance training, you need to make it uncomfortable for the dog. Push the inside of the cheek in between the rear teeth of the mouth and when the puppy bites down he will bite himself.

Another avoidance technique is to press your thumb down into the inside of its bottom jaw, with your remaining fingers holding the bottom of the jaw. It looks like the grip an angler would use to pull a fish out of the water by his mouth but don't pick the dog up this way, it is not a fish.

The third training method I recommend that can be used is to pick the puppy up by the scruff of the neck briefly, the way a mother dog would correct her pups. Make sure the pup is biting you when you do this.

Social Deprivation and extinction will also work for this problem. Since the puppy is trying to play and interact, remove your attention and stop playing for a short period of time when he bites you. Make an "ouch" noise to further get the point across. This will teach him that playing too rough means no playmate. If the puppy no longer receives the reward, the behavior will eventually become extinct.

Jumping

Your dog should be happy to see you when you arrive home, naturally you are happy to see them as well, and with all this excitement it is hard for your dog to not jump on you in excitement. This may be ok for you but your guests will probably not like it. If you pet your dog while it is jumping, you are rewarding the behavior, so please refrain from doing this. What you want to do is teach your dog to sit politely for greeting. There are a few methods of doing this which include Avoidance and Extinction.

With the avoidance method, there are two techniques that I recommend. The first method involves telling your dog to sit and following through with CCRR for the sit command; this should be done on leash. The other option is to use your houseline and step on it. When the dog jumps, it will correct itself if you are standing on the houseline. After the dog gets corrected tell the dog to sit and reinforce the command if needed. When using either method, it is important to give the dog plenty of praise so be sure to pet the dog while it is in the proper position.

Another avoidance training technique that has been used, involves kneeing the dog while the dog is jumping but without being able to force the dog into the correct position this method has its flaws.

Using extinction involves turning your back on the dog and ignoring the dog when it jumps on you. It is important that no one touches the dog during this training unless it is in the sitting position; otherwise, you are just rewarding the jumping and it will surely continue.

Using treats can work but the dog will select the reward of most value and your physical touch may be a greater reward than the treat for sitting.

Speak

Most dogs in the military are trained for bite work to give the dog the ability to take down or subdue an enemy on command. Sometimes a show of force is enough to scare an opponent into submission and the dog is not required to bite. To accomplish this, dogs can be taught to bark on command. My dog knew the command "WATCH 'EM" but any cue will elicit the same response if taught properly.

Teaching a dog to speak is tricky, not all dogs bark reliably on their own. You will need to find a trigger that causes the dog to bark such as a doorbell, someone knocking at the door, other dogs or any other thing that will cause your dog to bark. When you have a trigger that you can control, you are on your way.

Once your trigger and command are established, you will trigger the dog to bark while giving the command then praise, repeatedly. Once you have completed enough trials, the dog will automatically bark when it hears the cue. Gradually, reduce the amount of praise for the action on the reward schedule that is most appropriate for your dog's level of training.

Quiet

Once you have dogs that you can make bark, what about training one to be quiet? Being "QUIET" follows CCRR like so many other commands in this book, with that being said, you will tell the dog "QUIET" while it is barking and give it a few seconds to comply. If the dog does not stop barking, issue a correction. If the dog still does not comply, reinforce the command by applying steady, upward pressure on the slip collar; repeat the command until the dog stops barking and then release the pressure. Once the dog is "QUIET" be sure to praise enthusiastically.

Retrieving Objects

Training a dog to retrieve things is a fun and positive experience. This training is primarily reward based. First, we have to teach the dog to pick the item up. We will use a rope for our example. Waive the rope at the dog to incite the Prey Kill drive and as the dog is latching down on the object, give the dog a command such as "GET ROPE" then reward with either verbal, physical or food reward while repeating "GET ROPE" if the dog is not interested in the rope, you can shake the rope a little harder or hide it behind your back. If the dog lacks sufficient Prey Kill drive, you may gently open the dog's mouth and place the object in it. If you had to place the object, close the dog's mouth around it for a second or two then give the dog a high value reward. Once the dog is proficient at picking up the object, the second step is to get the dog to bring the item to you which is actually a separate command such as "COME".

After the dog knows how to pick up one object and bring it the handler, it is time to move on to the next object which could be anything such as your slippers, the newspaper or cold drink. Dogs may have an aversion to the taste of metal so attaching a toy to a metal object may help. There have been reports of dogs that have been trained to identify and retrieve over 700 individual objects. If you are going to train the dog to pick up multiple items, you will still use "GET " or "GET THE" as your command but the name of the object will change, just make sure that all items have distinct names so the dog can easily distinguish them from one another. How many are you going to teach your dog?

Away

We all love our dogs but begging is a horrible habit and sometimes we just need some space. To teach your dog the "AWAY" command, there are two options with the first option being Avoidance and

Reinforcement using the CCRR technique. This is the preferred method and starts with giving the dog the "AWAY" command, or any other cue you prefer. The second step is the correction. The third step is to apply physical pressure to the chain and basically remove the dog from the area while repeating the command. With my dog, the acceptable distance is about ten feet away. If the dog enters the space again, repeat the steps until the dog gets the idea.

The other way to accomplish this involves using positive reinforcement only with the use of a treat. I always prefer other options to treat training but hey it's your dog. To use treats for this task, you will first give the dog the command then lure it away to the appropriate area and reward the dog with the treat for compliance. I find the first method more effective but both can work.

Leave It

People often confuse "DROP IT" and "LEAVE IT" but in actuality they are two separate commands and should be treated as such. With this command, it also follows the CCRR structure. First, give the dog the command "LEAVE IT". If the dog continues to show interest in the item or distraction, then issue a correction in the most convenient direction. If the dog continues to go after it, pull the dog away with steady pressure and step in between the object and the dog if possible to block it. Timing is a little shorter with this command because it is important to not let the dog get the item which would be a reward and counterproductive to training.

This command can also be done with treats, although I prefer the method listed above. To use treats, you will simply give the dog the command and then distract the dog with a treat or other reward. When the dog is distracted feel free to give it the reward.

Dog Alarm Clock

Through the years, I have met many people who have a hard time waking up, this command is for them. Imagine if your dog helped wake you up in the morning. The dog could either lick your face or bark at you. Both methods rely on positive reward training. It requires that you pick an alarm tone and stick with it. It will become the cue for the dog to wake you up. When the alarm goes off get the dog to exhibit the desired behavior with either food or a verbal command and be sure to reward the dog heavily for exibiting the behavior. After enough trials the dog will display the desired response to the alarm without provacation.

To train the dog to lick you in the morning, peanut butter is useful.

Running on a Treadmill

Most people know a dog needs exercise just as much as we do; it is good for their health and wellbeing. An old cliché that trainers like to use is "A tired dog it a good dog" and this is true but unfortunately, due to environmental restrictions or time constraints a long walk may not always be possible. So why not train your dog to run on a treadmill? To accomplish this training, you will need to use a luring technique.

The handler uses a cue like "WALK" and guides the dog onto the treadmill with a leash while luring it with a treat; do not turn on the treadmill. Once the dog gets on the treadmill, give it the treat and repeat this process 20 to 40 times.

Once you have completed enough trials that the dog gets on the treadmill, turn it on the lowest setting while the dog is not on it and guide the dog onto the treadmill while repeating the command. Do several more trials at this speed then repeat the process and gradually reduce the number of treats you give the dog. Replace the food with verbal praise and petting. When the dog gets more experienced at using the treadmill start increasing the speed in small increments.

It is important to never tie your dog to the treadmill or leave it unattended as this could result in serious injury.

Relax

Training your dog to relax is a passive form of training which is done through positive reinforcement only. Wait for your dog to be silent and still then physically reward the dog while repeating the command "RELAX". If the dog starts getting overly excited immediately stop praising and ignore the dog. This training is best accomplished with little or no distraction. Once you have completed enough trials the dog will automatically relax when it hears the cue.

Aggression

Aggression itself is usually defined by "the intent to do harm". Many dogs will show "displays of aggression" such as barking, growling or snapping in the air which are considered distance-increasing actions, those which intend to get the person, dog or other perceived threat to move away. Some aggressive dogs display aggression that is mainly defensive and they will actually only bite if they perceive that they have no other option.

Yet other dogs may develop aggressive behavior due to medical reasons such as hormonal imbalances. Aggression is a common dog behavior and can be seen in all breeds of dogs, although some breeds have a predisposition to display such aggression. The breed standard usually spells out whether aggression is common in the breed and to what degree it is allowed. Individual dogs may or may not display the level of aggression that their breed standard suggests.

A dog's experiences may affect his chance of developing aggression. If a dog is attacked as a puppy it may develop fear-based dog aggression towards all dogs or perhaps only towards dogs that resemble the dog that attacked him. Do you remember the principal of one trial learning? It is important to note that a dog with dog-aggressive behavior does not necessarily show the same aggressive behavior towards humans. The two types of aggression are not necessarily related and do not always occur in the same animal.

Dog aggression often manifests between the ages of adolescence to social maturity which is from the ages of 6 months to 4 years. Warning signs such as fear or nervousness may only display under certain circumstances; while on leash, in the presence of food, in the presence of the owner, etc. or most commonly, over-the-top play behavior and can be seen at any stage of the dog's development.

Play behavior such as tackling, chasing, mouthing, nipping, pawing and wrestling are all normal canine behaviors that serve the evolutionary function of preparing the young dog for combat and hunting. Young dogs that engage in excessive amounts of these behaviors are much more likely to develop aggression as they age.

Dog-dog aggression should not be confused with dog-human aggression, also referred to as "Dominance Aggression" when directed at the owner. Many people commonly mistake fear and anxiety-related aggression as "Dominance Aggression" or "Alpha Confusion" which is inaccurate.

Lack of exercise is not a cause of aggressive behavior, although exercise boosts serotonin levels which offset stress hormones such as Cortisol and can complement a behavior modification program. However, it is a common belief that aggressive dogs are "not exercised enough." Many aggressive dogs are exercised regularly.

Alpha Confusion

The United States has the highest reported incidence of dog aggression problems of any country in the world, with an estimated 4.5 million dog attack victims each year. One of the major contributing factors to the development of dog aggression is living as part of a multi-dog household. More than a third of dogs in the United States live as part of multi-dog households. Another reason for this is that in America, a highly developed country, people often shower their dogs with affection and toys; leading to the dog believing that it is dominant and the leader of the pack. This could then lead to aggressive behavior. I like to call this "Alpha Confusion" which can also be referred to as "Dominace Aggression".

Lifestyles

Busy lifestyles are also a major contributing factor to the rising occurrences of aggression related attacks. As the American working week gets longer and longer, the responsibility of caring for their dogs often slips, causing mild and even more extreme cases of neglect. This neglect can start with something as simple as missing a walk here and there because of business meetings or late nights, neglect like that will eventually have an effect on the mental and/or physical well-being of the dog.

Separation Anxiety

Separation anxiety can be described as a condition when a dog exhibits distress and behavioral problems when separated from its handler. It is currently not completely understood why some dogs suffer from this behavior and others do not.

Separation Anxiety Causes

While there may be other causes of this condition, here are a few triggers that are pretty common.

If the dog is used to its handler, always being around or the team spending excessive amounts of time together, the dog may be too accustomed to human companionship and may exhibit issues when left alone.

If the dog has a traumatic event or one the dog percieves as traumatic like being abandoned by a previous owner, time at a shelter, being left at a boarding facility or some other similar event can cause this condition.

A change in the pack structure at home can also create this issue such as the loss of a family member or other pet whether by death or long term separation.

Separation Anxiety Behaviors

There are a lot of behaviors that can be associated with separation anxiety. This list is not all inclusive but here are a few behaviors to watch for.

Urinating and Defecating – A dog that has been properly housetrained does not usually have accidents unless it has gone for an extended period of time without sufficient time for relief. If the dog urinates or defecates in front of you it is most likely a dominance issue. It is most likely separation anxiety if the dog does it while separated from its handler.

Barking or Howling – Is another characteristic of this behavior and occurs when separated from its handler. If the dog hears a noise that triggers the howling such as other dogs vocalizing or even sirens, then it is most likely not separation anxiety.

Destructive Behaviors – Some of the things that fall into this category are issues such as adult dogs chewing on furniture, walls, window sills or other property. They may also exhibit digging up plants or simply big holes in the yard. These issues can be problematic, not only for the destruction of your property but also because the dog may actually cause itself physical injury.

Coprophagia – This one is pretty gross but it occurs and can be defined as a dog that consumes its own feces, either partially or entirely while during the period of separation.

Pacing – Some dogs will follow the same path incessantly while you are away which could be a straight line or a circular pattern but it is always repetitive and occurs while you are gone.

Escaping – Well balanced dogs are ok with being separated for a period of time but if they try to escape confinement by digging, scratching, jumping or climbing barriers the dog most likely has issues with separation anxiety.

Working with Separation Anxiety

With mild separation anxiety there are a variety of things that can be done but the most common ones involve using puzzle toys filled with food or treats to keep the dog occupied while the owner is gone, this is called "Counter Conditioning". Dog owners dealing with separation anxiety can also try changing one or more parts of their exit routine so there is not a distinct pattern for the dog to fixate on such as always putting your shoes on, grabbing your jacket, then the keys and always doing it in the same order. The owner should instead try to vary their routines prior to leaving. Try putting your shoes on and reading a book or some other activity instead of leaving. Grab your keys but do not go anywhere. Behaviors like this can effectively alleviate anxiety because the dog is not expecting you to leave, based on a specific set of cues.

Moderate to Severe Separation Anxiety – This is more time consuming to work on and can involve intensive "Counter Conditioning". Treatment progress and behavior can often be a difficult read for the untrained person. I recommend finding an expert in your area to help you design and help monitor an appropriate course of action. Do not punish or correct your dog for separation anxiety because it is not caused by disobedience or spite. The behavior is a distress response and correction based training will most likely make the situation worse.

Separation Anxiety Training Techniques

When you begin training try to start with the "STAY"command while insight and then use advanced "STAY" techniques to progress to staying while you are out of site. Start by using an interior door. Then gradually work on doors that exit the house.

Before you begin, you need to establish the amount of time it takes for the dog to exhibit the behavior. Often in the beginning this will be almost immediate upon your departure or you leaving the dog's line of sight. If it takes ten minutes before the dog becomes anxious, consider it lucky. In either case, this amount of time is your baseline time.

Once you have established your baseline time, decrease it by one minute or a few seconds, depending on the situation and reward the dog for not exhibiting the behavior. Once you have completed 8 trials, increase the time and continue training. If you find that the increase is too much, go back to the last known length of time and repeat the process 8 more times. Continue this process until the dog can endure a longer separation without an issue.

During the training process be sure to wait a few minutes before departing again and do not depart while the dog is anything but calm. If you leave too soon or before he calms down, this could lead to a failure during the next trial.

Remember to not make a big deal of your leaving or arriving back when training. Do not get overly excited during your greeting or departure as this may make the problem worse.

This training takes a long time to accomplish and requires lots of training and can take several weeks, depending on severity. Once your dog can tolerate half an hour or more of separation then you may increase the amount of time being separated by larger quantities and increasing time gradually, by a few minutes each time. Once the dog is good for ninety minutes or more, it is likely the dog will be able to endure several hours of continuous separation.

Other Alternatives for Separation Anxiety

1) Take the dog with you.

2) Have someone watch your dog.

3) Take your dog to a dog sitter or a doggy daycare.

4) Crating the dog may or may not work, if the dog views its crate as safe place then it may be comforting to the dog. For some dogs it can be more stressful. You will need to judge if this solution is right for your dog.

5) Exercise the dog prior to leaving. This will wear the dog out so it goes to sleep.

6) Ask your vet if medications may be helpful if all else fails.

Behaviors that are not separation anxiety

Sometimes, people mistake separation anxiety for other issues. Here is a list of things to keep in mind that may seem like separation anxiety but are not.

Incomplete Potty Training– A dog that occasionally urinates or defecates in the house while the owner is not watching may have been trained improperly which can manifest when an owner makes

the dog afraid to eliminate in front of them with improperly timed corrections or punishments.

Boredom – Dogs are relatively smart and can get bored easily. If they are bored, they will find something to occupy their time which may lead to destructive behaviors as a form of entertainment. This behavior can often be curbed by providing the dog with an activity such as foraging for food or working to receive a treat like putting peanut butter in a dog toy that forces the dog to work for the content.

Incontinence – Incontinence can be caused by medical conditions and as a result of medical procedures such as spaying, bladder stones, kidney disease, Cushing's disease, neurological disorders or even abnormalities in the genitals. Some medication will also cause this condition, if your dog is on a new medication please contact your vet to see if this may be a factor. Incontinence can also be caused by old age, a urinary tract infection or it could be hormone related. This behavior is best described as a dog that eliminates its bladder while resting and often is not aware of the elimination. If you believe it may be one of these issues, please see your veterinarian.

Submissive or Excitement Urination – Dogs that urinate while displaying submissive positions such as flattening the ears back, crouching, holding the tail low or rolling over to display the belly is called submissive urination and can be exhibited during greetings, play, physical contact or while being reprimanded. These behaviors are not attributed to separation anxiety and can be reduced by a change in the owner's behavior such as toning down excitement during play, waiting a few minutes prior to greeting the dog or reducing the level of correction issued to the dog for undesirable behavior or disobedience.

Marking – Sometimes dogs leave scent marks in the house by urinating small amounts on surfaces that are vertical like a couch or wall and the behavior is often accompanied by the dog raising a leg regardless of gender. Directly correcting the dog for this behavior may not be the best course of action as you may simply be training the dog to do it while you are not looking which will make it even harder to curb. Instead of a correction, you want to catch the dog prior to doing it and disrupt the behavior with play or some other suitable distraction. It will be easiest to do this if you observe the behavior and look for signs that the dog is preparing to mark such as sniffing around. Your dog should already be familiar with the things in your house so sniffing is a good indication that marking may occur soon. If you see your dog getting ready to mark take the dog outside and if it marks outdoors, then reward the dog heavily. Make it more rewarding to go outside than inside and if the dog goes more often outside than in, you are well on your way to correcting the behavior.

Dogs will often mark in the same spot because the odor can trigger the behavior. If you suspect your dog of marking in the house, it is vital to clean the spot thoroughly to eliminate the odor as to not trigger the behavior in the future. There are several specialized products and or home remedies that can be used to totally eliminate the odor, thus reducing the temptation to mark in the same spot. Never use ammonia based product because urine contains ammonia and may trigger the behavior.

Juvenile Destruction – Most dogs under the age of two are prone to exhibiting destructive behavior with or without the owners' presence. This behavior is normal and can be fixed by proper crate training. Please refer to the crate training and house breaking section of this book.

"Ivy"

Conclusion

Congratulations! You made it most of the way through this book. You should be more educated about dog training than 99% of the population. Be sure to re-read the information until you understand it fully. The information in this book should be helpful in assisting you with all of your training, both basic and advanced and I am glad I could provide it to you. If you remember these techniques and apply them to your dog on a regular basis, you should have the best behaved dog on the block. You will be more successful if you take your time to learn the techniques and apply them correctly, in a calm and relaxed state of mind. Everything runs down leash and if you try to train your dog while you are frustrated, you will only prolong the entire training process. If anyone asks you how your dog became so well behaved, I hope you mention me and as always happy training.

Louis William Robinson and "Sadie"

Dog Training Journal Entry's

The information in this material will give you valuable insight into common dog training problems. There are many great pointers and things to watch out for. The bonus section is a portion of my Dog Training Journal (DTJ) in which an entire years worth of my dog training thoughts are recorded. Keep an eye out for the rest of the DJT when it is released in the near future. www.robinsondogtraining.com/ebook.html

11/30/2008

Today, I worked with several dogs. My first appointment was working with a service dog. Her owner is Bi-Polar. She needs her dog to help her with general day to day functions. The dog is approximately 5 weeks through the 10 weeks of training. Her dog was already pretty advanced for what I normally see and was doing well. This dog is a 2 year old, chocolate lab named Sweet Pea. Sweet Pea met my dog Lucy for the first time and they got along so well. Because her owner was not able to apply a physical correction that was meaningful to the dog, I decided to introduce her to the concept of an electronic collar. Both the dog and the owner seemed to take to the idea fairly well.

My next appointment was a group class and I showed them how to make their dog heel, properly. It seems the entire class was able to grasp the sit concept that was introduced, fairly well from last week and has progressed as scheduled. We also went over the 2nd week test with them and everyone was applying the technique appropriately.

My last appointment of the evening was a therapy dog named Mini. She is being trained to assist children during dental procedures, to reduce or eliminate the necessity for pain killers. We had to cut our session short tonight because the owner got a cactus stuck in her thigh. Overall the training is still going as scheduled and I don't have much more to elaborate on.

12/01/2008

I had 2 sessions today. The first session was with a pair of older German Shepherds that have been through several other trainers. Their names are "Ginger and Zeus" they are fairly well behaved but only listen when they want to. I have taught the owners how to properly use a choke chain and they are still perfecting the timing and the technique. They wanted to see if I could handle the dogs while walking by a yard with a Pitt Bull that likes to hang over the wall and bark. When customers want to see a demonstration such as this I am always glad to oblige. I took one dog and walked near the Pit Bull by issuing a couple of good corrections before Zeus began to ignore the distraction. They were astounded and then asked me to show them with Ginger who was often the agitator. I joyfully demonstrated with Ginger and produced the same result to their amazement. They then challenged me to walk by with both dogs since they often feed off of each other's energy and get all wound up. Both dogs did beautifully and my technique prevailed once again. After they have the obedience nailed down, they will move to protection.

My next appointment was with a couple who bought 2 baby Shepherds and want to eventually progress into protection. Before we can do that, we need to cover all of the basics first. The dogs are about six months old and the male seems like he has a low titration level. The dog's titration level will probably increase with age but currently my evaluation is that he is what I often refer to as a soft dog. It will be fun to mold such a young pup into a family protector and it will be very rewarding.

12/2/2008

Today I volunteered day at the pound, I usually do adoptions but sometimes I give advice and last week I did some temperament testing on a Neapolitan Mastiff named Monster. The director of the pound asked for my opinion on the dog because she wanted to know if I thought he was a liability. After spending some time with the dog I deemed him adoptable and he was adopted the next day. While I was there, today, I got a phone call from a gentleman asking for sessions geared towards protection. He did not own a dog yet but was interested in hiring me. I told him that since I was at the pound, I would look for a suitable dog for the job.

The first dog I saw was a 4 year old, male Rottweiler. I took this dog out to the play area to check his prey drive and was very disappointed to see that he was not interested in the ball or Frisbee. In a high stress environment such as the pound it is often hard to test for this drive but since my client requested a guard dog, I was not comfortable with this dog due to the lack of prey drive.

After putting this dog up, I took another look around and was shocked to find a 1 year old, female Malinois. She was labeled as a shepherd mix but was clearly a Malinois. This is my favorite breed of dog and she was very well mannered. I took her out to check her prey drive and she passed with flying colors. I immediately called my new customer and told him to come right away because a dog of this caliber is not going to last long. He arrived and hour later and adopted the dog. We set up his first training day for the next day. I also found a home for a kitten before I left.

12/03/2008
Today was my first appointment working with the Malinois. The dogs' new owner is former military and this was his main reason for hiring me. I went through my normal first session with him and both he and the dog picked up the concepts and training very well. I have no doubt that both the dog and owner will have a blast doing the training.

12/06/08

I met with my customer who wants to train her dogMini for therapy to use in her own dental practice in the future. We did an impromptu trial at the mall, down the road from her house. It did not go well because the dog was too distracted to work at a level that I felt was reliable. I instructed her to work daily with her dog in similar locations for the next week and hopefully she will be able to pass the American Kennel Club Canine Good Citizen evaluation. If she works hard this week it can be accomplished.

I also met with my service dog today that has nowbeen in the house for a total of three weeks. The dog is adjusting well and naturally exhibits a lot of behaviors that we were looking for. Now the trick is to get her to do it reliably. This dog should be a breeze to train due to her age and temperament.

Last appointment of the evening was with "Jack" the protection dog. This is one of the hardest biting dogs I have encountered. We have transitioned to a hidden sleeve and a plastic fist for hand protection. This dog often goes for the hand so I figured that hand protection was a good idea. During the first bite attempt, the dog released the bite prior to being instructed to do so and began looking for something softer to bite. He almost got my non protected arm. I instructed the owner to take the dog outdoors in order to have more room to work and get the dog used to holding onto the new equipment. After several bites, I realized that I needed to wear a leather gauntlet under the bite sleeve and took a break to put it on. Once this was accomplished, we moved back inside and continued with the home invasion protection training.

12/07/08

One of my group class customers opted to get her last three sessions as private sessions. I visited her and her yellow lab "Daisy", today. She said the dog was out of control but when I arrived all that I observed was normal puppy behavior. She was having a hard time getting her dog to do basic commands. Upon evaluation of her technique, I found several things wrong. Her timing was off, the correction was too delicate and the leash was usually tight when she tried to administer a correction. We spent about 40 minutes working on her technique.

Second appointment was with my service dog in the 5th week of training. She had begun complaining about her dog's behavior slipping so I did a technique evaluation and found her timing to be off. We went over the timing information that is presented in the first lesson and got her back on track. She noticed an immediate turnaround in the dog's behavior.

My last appointment was the group class' 3rd lesson. Again, the timing was wrong and I spent time going over that information as well as teaching the down command. We spent 30 minutes practicing the technique before we applied it to the dogs. The dogs all listened to me, but knew they could get away with not responding to their owners. It was an eye opener for the owners to see the difference in behavior when I had the leash and they all vowed to work harder at their timing.

12/08/08

My morning customers were complaining about not being able to control their large shepherds while out on a walk. We covered heel last week so I thought they just needed a little fine tuning. I wanted to duplicate the situation in order for me to show them how to keep the dogs under control. We went to the dog park near their house. To my delight there were several dogs there and I got to demonstrate the technique in a situation the dogs would normally misbehave. The owners were astounded at the difference a few good corrections could have on the dog. After a couple of corrections, the dogs were paying attention to my lead and not worrying about the distractions. After I showed them what was possible, I focused on the owners' technique and found the source of the problem. The issue was with the application of last week's lesson as well as the timing. After leaving this appointment I checked my voicemail and realized the next appointment had gone into labor and needed to cancel so I headed home for a couple hours, until my final appointment of the evening.

My final appointment is with a woman on a fixed budget who requested short sessions, focused on the heel. Her sessions are only supposed to be about fifteen minutes long. I met with her and her dog and had him heeling in about three minutes. It took the other twelve minutes for me to properly demonstrate the technique. I will meet with her again tomorrow after I visit the pound.

12/09/08

Went to the pound this morning and when I arrived I realized that I was the only adoptions counselor there. With four people waiting for someone to show dogs. It took me about an hour to get all of the people taken care of and then my help arrived. We continued to be busy throughout the shift and I managed to do a total of seven adoptions. While I was on shift, I inquired about the status of my coupon distribution and found both locations to be out so I made copies and took them back.

Second appointment with the heel lady and she seems pleased with the progress that is being made and says she has been practicing on her foot, like I demonstrated. I'm not certain she was actually doing the exercise because her technique was still off, but then again, it took me longer than a day to learn it as well. We went for a walk and I handled both dogs at the same time to show her what it looked like.

12/10/2008

My first appointment this morning was with a young border collie that was almost given away. The customer called me a few days ago to tell me that his wife was at her wits end with the dog's behavior. Apparently, she has never had a high energy pup before or any dog for that matter and could not deal with the rough play. I observed and what I saw was normal puppy behavior which can be scary for someone with small kids and no dog experience. The husband did not want to give the dog away and I didn't feel it was necessary either. I told him that if her biggest concern was the rough play with the children while she is trying to get out the door for her day, with the kids, then they should consider getting an electronic collar so that she does not have to chase after the dog in order to issue a correction. They seemed to take to the idea pretty well so we will see how this goes. Maybe this pup can stay in its home after all.

I went to see my next client and his beautiful Malinois this morning and the dog is as beautiful as ever. He has the sit command at about an 80% level with no distractions. We went for our first walk with the heel command. The owner did ok but needs a little work on the timing. During our walk, he realized that my correction was more of a snap and related that he had been pulling instead of snapping. This will make a huge difference in the effectiveness of the training. We were supposed to be doing snake aversion next week but I decided that it will be too cold to get an active snake and I do not want the dog to fear me when we transition into protection work. We will wait on the aversion training until the last session.

12/11/2008

I only had one appointment today. It was the woman who requested the 15 minute lessons. Again, I handled both of her dogs and everything went well. She may have to give up the dog because she believes she may be allergic. She has decided to continue her lessons at a later date.

12/12/2008

My morning appointment was with 6 month old German Shepherd Puppy named "Luger". His owner had been previously trained by another company. At the end of their training, the other trainer told the client that the methods she taught him were not the same methods that she had used on her own dog. I'm not sure why anyone would teach something that they don't practice. After evaluation of "Luger", my opinion is that he needs a lot of work. With my methods, I will be able to get him into shape in no time. The owner took to the lesson well and the dog did a good job too.

12/13/2008

I worked on my favorite dog today, "Jack", as usual he was more than happy to bite me. A small animal crawled into the customer's roof and died. The smell was awful but it was not too unbearable to deal with so the training went ahead on schedule. Sometimes, Jack gets too excited to do the work and bypasses rooms without sniffing. In order to fix this problem, we had Jack do a few blank problems with no decoy. He seemed to be looking a little harder after a few of these drills so we will be progressing the training with this exercise to solve this problem.

12/14/2008

Group class only had 1 customer show today so I got to focus a little harder on the individual issues she was having and give her more in depth explanation.

12/15/2008

Sweet Pea is doing well with the grab it command and showing a much higher level of prey kill drive. Her owner has been instructed to make the transition to the cell phone alarm as the trigger and I watched her apply the technique to the dog. Her method was timed well and the dog is right on schedule.

I was supposed to do an American Kennel Club Canine Good Citizen evaluation today but due to bad weather it has been rescheduled for a later date.

Test 1

1. How does a mother dog correct her pups?
   A) Grounds them.
   B) Licks them.
   C) Picks them up by the scruff of the neck.
   D) Gives them a pat on the head.

2. If a dog's chain is too heavy, it can do what?
   A) Weigh the dog down.
   B) Make other dogs envious.
   C) Make the dog more confident.
   D) Make him listen more.

3. When is it ok to leave the training collar on the dog?
   A) Sometimes
   B) Never
   C) Under supervision

4. How can you tell if the training collar fits properly?
   A) It slips easily over the head.
   B) It hangs low on the chest.
   C) The dog has difficulty breathing.
   D) It drags on the ground.

5. What letter should the chain resemble with the dog facing you when put on correctly?
   A) d
   B) b
   C) p

6. What type of collar should every dog have?
   A) Buckle
   B) Rhinestone
   C) Pincher
   D) Spray

7. How many fingers should fit between the slip collar of a large dog?
   A) 1
   B) 2
   C) 3

8. What is the proper order of commands and actions to train the dog?
   A) Command, Correction, Reinforcement, Reward.
   B) Correction, Command, Praise, Reinforcement.
   C) Praise, Command, Correction, Reinforcement.
   D) Reinforcement, Command, Correction, Praise.

9. How many corrections are considered animal abuse?
   A) 1
   B) 2
   C) 3
   D) 4

10. What is the training collar designed to do?
    A) Briefly tighten
    B) Look pretty
    C) Punish the dog
    D) Reward the dog.

Test 2

1) In order to generate a Conditioned Response two stimuli have to be paired in how many seconds?
   A) 0-.5
   B) 1-2
   C) 3-4
   D) 5-10

2) The process of extinction occurs when:
   A) The ABC and EFG are no longer paired.
   B) The VFR and FR are no longer paired
   C) The CS and UCS are no longer paired.
   D) The UCS and UCR are no longer paired.

3) Method of Successive Approximation means:
   A) Changing the reward schedule.
   B) Moving from simple to complex.
   C) Training the dog for success.
   D) Training the dog to leave the area.

4) What does Stimulus Discrimination mean?
   A) The dog does not like a particular command.
   B) The dog thinks that two stimuli sound the same.
   C) Two commands sound the similar.
   D) Two commands that sound different.

5) What is Luring?
   A) Training a dog with a choke chain.
   B) Training a dog with treats or toys.

C) Training a dog on a boat.

D) Training a dog with an electronic collar.

6) What is Avoidance Training?

A) The dog learns in order to get a treat.

B) The dog learns in order to get rest.

C) The dog learns in order to get a pat on the head.

D) The dog learns in order to evade discomfort.

7) How old should a dog be before training off leash?

A) 14 weeks old

B) 6 months old

C) 1 year old

D) 2 years old

8) What is the best example of One Trial Learning?

A) A drug dog that burns his nose on a motorcycle tail pipe.

B) A pet dog that sits immediately for a treat.

C) A service dog that pick up an item upon first request.

D) A barking dog that is immediately silent when given the command "Quiet".

9) Variable Reward Schedule comes after the dog is proficient at what schedule?

A) Variable Interval Reward

B) Fixed Ratio

C) Fixed Interval Reward

D) Continuous Reinforcement Schedule

10) What is Escape Training?

A) A technique used to keep a dog within a specific boundary.

B) A technique used to help the handler leave a difficult situation.

C) A technique used to guide a dog into the correct position.

D) A technique your dog uses to get out of his kennel.

Test Answers

Test 1

1. C
2. A
3. C
4. A
5. C
6. A
7. B
8. A
9. C
10. A

Test 2

1. A
2. C
3. B
4. D
5. B
6. D
7. D
8. A
9. B
10. C

Training Curriculum Guidelines

The curriculum on the following page is only a suggestion. Train at your own pace. Train your dog for a minimum of 5 to 10 minutes twice per day. For faster results, I recommend training your dog more frequently. Keep your training sessions less than 20 minutes, even when working on multiple commands. If training multiple times a day, be sure to give your dog equal training time to break time which could be rest or play. The exception is if you are training during a walk or conducting more advanced training that requires traveling as part of the training such as "HEEL", Scent Detection, or Tracking techniques which are not covered in this book. In the military, when doing detection training we trained no more than 20 minutes at a time, otherwise the dog would become bored, decreasing motivation and reliability. Dogs have short attention spans.

When you first begin training, do no more than 3 new commands per week. Keep track of one command per dog log sheet in order to easily see your progress. Never stop working on old commands entirely, only reduce the frequency of trials.

Begin training with basic obedience commands that lack a proficiency of 80 percent, based on your personal evaluation. If your dog does not know how to sit or its name, then that is your starting point. The curriculum on the following page is only a suggested order of importance and can be modified depending on your dog's needs.

Always remember that anything you do with your dog is training. Any interaction is training, regardless as to if it is intentional or not. Your dog is constantly observing and learning from you. If you tell your dog to do something you must follow through even if you are not in a dedicated training session.

"Lucy"

Sample Curriculum

This curriculum is only a suggestion. Train at your own pace.

Week 1
- Read the book
- Foot Drills
- Learn Come
- Learn Sit
- Homework Assignment: Foot drills, Come and Sit, Complete test # 1

Week 2
- Learn boundary control techniques
- Learn "Heel" technique (walking)
- Learn "Heel" (Stationary)
- Homework assignment: Foot Drills, Boundary Control, Heel, Heel Stationary

Week 3
- Learn Down
- Homework assignment: All previous commands, "Down", Complete Test # 2

Week 4
- Learn Stay Techniques
- Homework Assignment: Work on all previous commands and add "Stay"

Week 5
- Learn Obedience drill's and patterns
- Move to Variable Interval Reward schedule with "Stay"
- Move to Variable Frequency Reward schedule (previous commands)
- Learn Advanced "Stay" Techniques
- Homework assignment: Work on "Obedience Drills" and Advanced "Stay"

Week 6 - X
Pick new commands or increase your intervals and continue training at your own pace. There is no limit to the things you can train your dog to do.

Dog Log Instructions

Tracking progress is an important step in dog training and ensures that the dog is progressing as scheduled. The "Dog Log" forms are at the end of this book and are designed for you to keep track of your progress.

In the Task collumn write down the command you are keeping track of for the week. Then write down your start time and move to the first trial. Begin the trial by giving your dog the command.

If the dog responds correctly to the command the first time, then you will mark yes in the box by the appropriate trial number. If the dog does not respond correctly, apply a correction, either verbal or physical, and place a no in the appropriate box. This will complete 1 trial continue this until you complete trial number 10. Finish your training session by writing the end time in the last section.

You will notice that during the training process the amount of "No's" will decrease as the training progresses. Keep the training sessions short in order to ensure the dog does not get bored.

I recommend a <u>minimum</u> of 2 short training sessions per day. Additional sessions will yeild superior performance.

Louis William Robinson and "Lucy"

Dog Log Forms

ROBINSON DOG TRAINING PERFORMANCE EVALUATION FORM (DOG LOG)

RDT K-9 TEAM

Start Date:
End Date:
Your Name:
Dogs Name:
Dogs Age:
Dogs Sex:

Command List

(C)	= (Come)
(S)	= (Sit)
(HS) =	(Heel Stationary)
(D)	= (Down)
(T)	= (Stay)

Notes:

Weekly Results

Command	Start Time	Day	Trial 1	Trial 2	Trial 3	Trial 4	Trial 5	Trial 6	Trial 7	Trial 9	Trial 10	End Time	Notes:
		Day 1											
		Day 1a											
		Day 2											
		Day 2a											
		Day 3											
		Day 4a											
		Day 5											
		Day 5a											
		Day 6											
		Day 6a											
		Day 7											
		Day 7a											

Additional Notes:

NOTES:

ROBINSON DOG TRAINING PERFORMANCE EVALUATION FORM (DOG LOG)

RDT K-9

Start Date: _____
End Date: _____
Your Name: _____
Dogs Name: _____
Dogs Age: _____
Dogs Sex: _____

Notes: _____

Command List

(C) = (Come)
(S) = (Sit)
(HS) = (Heel Stationary)
(D) = (Down)
(T) = (Stay)

Weekly Results

Command	Start Time	Day	Trial 1	Trial 2	Trial 3	Trial 4	Trial 5	Trial 6	Trial 7	Trial 9	Trial 10	End Time	Notes:
		Day 1											
		Day 1a											
		Day 2											
		Day 2a											
		Day 3											
		Day 4a											
		Day 5											
		Day 5a											
		Day 6											
		Day 6a											
		Day 7											
		Day 7a											

Additional Notes:

NOTES:

RDT K-9

ROBINSON DOG TRAINING PERFORMANCE EVALUATION FORM (DOG LOG)

Start Date:

End Date:

Your Name:

Dogs Name:

Dogs Age:

Dogs Sex:

Command List

(C)	=	(Come)
(S)	=	(Sit)
(HS)	=	(Heel Stationary)
(D)	=	(Down)
(T)	=	(Stay)

Notes:

Weekly Results

Command	Start Time	Day	Trial 1	Trial 2	Trial 3	Trial 4	Trial 5	Trial 6	Trial 7	Trial 9	Trial 10	End Time	Notes:
		Day 1											
		Day 1a											
		Day 2											
		Day 2a											
		Day 3											
		Day 4a											
		Day 5											
		Day 5a											
		Day 6											
		Day 6a											
		Day 7											
		Day 7a											

Additional Notes:

NOTES:

155

Robinson Dog Training Performance Evaluation Form (DOG LOG)

RDT K-9

Start Date:
End Date:
Your Name:
Dogs Name:
Dogs Age:
Dogs Sex:

Command List

(C)	=	(Come)
(S)	=	(Sit)
(HS)	=	(Heel Stationary)
(D)	=	(Down)
(T)	=	(Stay)

Notes:

Weekly Results

Command	Start Time	Day	Trial 1	Trial 2	Trial 3	Trial 4	Trial 5	Trial 6	Trial 7	Trial 9	Trial 10	End Time	Notes:
		Day 1											
		Day 1a											
		Day 2											
		Day 2a											
		Day 3											
		Day 4a											
		Day 5											
		Day 5a											
		Day 6											
		Day 6a											
		Day 7											
		Day 7a											

Additional Notes:

NOTES:

ROBINSON DOG TRAINING PERFORMANCE EVALUATION FORM (DOG LOG)

RDT K-9 TEAMS

Start Date:
End Date:
Your Name:
Dogs Name:
Dogs Age:
Dogs Sex:

Command List
(C)   = (Come)
(S)   = (Sit)
(HS) = (Heel Stationary)
(D)   = (Down)
(T)   = (Stay)

Notes:

Weekly Results

Command	Start Time	Day	Trial 1	Trial 2	Trial 3	Trial 4	Trial 5	Trial 6	Trial 7	Trial 9	Trial 10	End Time	Notes:
		Day 1											
		Day 1a											
		Day 2											
		Day 2a											
		Day 3											
		Day 4a											
		Day 5											
		Day 5a											
		Day 6											
		Day 6a											
		Day 7											
		Day 7a											

Additional Notes:

NOTES:

Robinson Dog Training Performance Evaluation Form (DOG LOG)

RDT K-9

Start Date:
End Date:
Your Name:
Dogs Name:
Dogs Age:
Dogs Sex:

Command List

(C) = (Come)
(S) = (Sit)
(HS) = (Heel Stationary)
(D) = (Down)
(T) = (Stay)

Notes:

Weekly Results

Command	Start Time	Day	Trial 1	Trial 2	Trial 3	Trial 4	Trial 5	Trial 6	Trial 7	Trial 9	Trial 10	End Time	Notes
		Day 1											
		Day 1a											
		Day 2											
		Day 2a											
		Day 3											
		Day 4a											
		Day 5											
		Day 5a											
		Day 6											
		Day 6a											
		Day 7											
		Day 7a											

Additional Notes:

NOTES:

ROBINSON DOG TRAINING PERFORMANCE EVALUATION FORM (DOG LOG)

RDT K-9

Start Date:

End Date:

Your Name:

Dogs Name:

Dogs Age:

Dogs Sex:

Notes:

Command List

(C) = (Come)
(S) = (Sit)
(HS) = (Heel Stationary)
(D) = (Down)
(T) = (Stay)

Weekly Results

Command	Start Time	Day	Trial 1	Trial 2	Trial 3	Trial 4	Trial 5	Trial 6	Trial 7	Trial 9	Trial 10	End Time	Notes
		Day 1											
		Day 1a											
		Day 2											
		Day 2a											
		Day 3											
		Day 4a											
		Day 5											
		Day 5a											
		Day 6											
		Day 6a											
		Day 7											
		Day 7a											

Additional Notes:

NOTES:

Contact Information

My services include puppy school, obedience, agility, problem solving/prevention, executive protection, guard, rattle, handicapped assistance training and certification, therapy, search and rescue, dog safety, care, crate training, and house breaking. I even offer K-9 tactical training and decoy training consultations to civilian police departments around the globe. Creating cooperative canines is my business. I love this job!

I offer private training and video training worldwide. Check out the website for more details.

Contact Information

Website: www.robinsondogtraining.com

Email: info@robinsondogtraining.com

Facebook: facebook.com/robinsondogtraining

Louis William Robinson
and "Sadie" 2013

Made in the USA
San Bernardino, CA
28 March 2017